WHAT PEOP

"If you think and don't act BOLD, ⌐
head."   r

~ Shared on behalf of **Gary Keller**
Co-Founder and Chairman of Keller WIlliams Realty, Inc.
#1 New York Times Bestselling Author

"We are a community service organization that just so happens to sell real estate."

~ **Matt Hermes**
Hermes Realtor Group

"Knowing your worth means that you have taken the significance journey going from survival to success to significance and finally becoming a transformational leader. Gary Keller has taught us to become the leaders that we need to be to attract the talent that we want. Attracting great talent, along with a vision that allows your business to get as big as it needs to get, to insure everyone to gets what they want! For me and KCN, that meant more than selling homes, it means transforming lives. The strategic giving of Kristan's Home of Hope, allows us to have experiences worth giving!"

~ **Kristan Cole**
Kristan Cole Real Estate Network, Kristan's Home of Hope

"KW has been built by the agents, FOR the agents."

~ **Lance Loken**
Chief Executive Officer, The Loken Group

"Keller Williams not only encourages you, but teaches you to how to put a plan in place so that you can CHOOSE to work in five years or less, by building passive streams of income through profit-share, team-building, and real estate investments. Now I truly have a Life Worth Living, can give Experiences Worth Giving and leave a positive impact on everyone in my life."

~ **Dina Mitchell**
Managing Director of KW Brokerages for Caleb Hayes Enterprises

"It's not just about what you 'get' at KW . . . it's about who you become!"

~ **Aaron Kaufman**
Keller Williams Growth Coach

"The most impactful lesson about money that I have learned is that the greatest joy comes from giving."

~ **Mo Anderson**
Vice Chairman, Keller WIlliams Realty, Inc.

The colleagues and authors of "Knowing Worth"

"When you have self-worth,

you can give that gift to

someone else."

~ Kim Rogne

KNOWING
WORTH

Stories Gathered By:
Kim Rogne

These stories are based on the experiences of individuals. Every effort has been made to ensure the accuracy of content.

For information about KNOWING WORTH
Or Keller Williams – Miwaukee Southwest
Please contact Kim Rogne at:
414-510-9938 | krogne@kw.com

Knowing Worth
Authors: Kim Rogne, Dave Bruno, Julia Kellogg, Scott Klaas, Jill LeCount, Terri Lewis, Michelle Mueller, Brad Parent, Janet Ruffolo, Jeremy Rynders, Delisa Yaeger

Publication Coordinator: Kim Rogne
Book Cover Design: Michael Nicloy, www.nico11publishing.com
Contributing Editor and Interior Layout: Reji Laberje, Signature Strength, www.bucketlisttobookshelf.com
Author Photos: Kimberly Laberge, http://labergekimberly.wixsite.com/thedramaden
Photos are provided by and used with permission of the contributing authors.

First Printing: 2019
Printed and bound in the United States of America.

DEDICATION:

For everyone who has had an experience worth giving. Your stories are a powerful force; share and use them for good.

"Success isn't just about

what you accomplish in life,

it's about what you inspire

others to do."

~ ZeroDean.com

YOUR STORIES OF WORTH

INSPIRED BY THE KELLER WILLIAMS MISSION:

CAREERS WORTH HAVING.

BUSINESSES WORTH OWNING.

LIVES WORTH LIVING.

EXPERIENCES WORTH GIVING.

LEGACIES WORTH LEAVING.

.

Kim Rogne, Team Leader of Keller Williams Milwaukee Southwest, teaches agents in-person and online about the subject of self-worth.

Worth

◆ ◆ ◆

"Self-esteem is what you think, and feel, and believe about yourself. Self-worth is recognizing you are greater than all of those things."

*That's what I wanted this project to be. No matter what we each wrote about, I wanted every person, including the readers, to leave this experience truly owning self-**worth**. Careers worth having, businesses worth owning, lives worth living, experiences worth giving, and legacies worth leaving can't happen if we don't embody self-worth. It's not just words or affirmations; we must KNOW WORTH. When you have self-worth, you can give that gift to someone else. The gift is delivered through the power of stories. People can read these real-life experiences of successful people, see themselves, and increase their own self-worth.*

May these true stories provide abundance and inspiration to all who read them.

"Be fearless in the pursuit of

what sets your soul on fire."

~ *Jennifer Lee*

CAREER

❖ ❖ ❖

A career worth having is when you are recognized as an expert in your industry by your clients, colleagues, and other professionals. It is a compass to a fulfilling and prosperous life. You work in synergy and discover your value while advancing your skills and talents through the best training and systems available.

In Keller Williams Realty, they value God first, family second, and then business. That speaks volumes.

Careers should be challenging, rewarding, and full of opportunities. It's ideal to be surrounded by like-mind individuals encouraging one another to set goals, dream big, and accomplish the impossible.

A career is truly worth having when it propels you to jump out of bed in the morning, empowered and unstoppable.

"I've learned that people will

forget what you said, people

will forget what you did, but

people will never forget how

you made them feel."

~ Maya Angelou

Janet Ruffolo *is an avid Realtor who helps sellers, buyers, and investors. She specializes in helping homeowners avoid foreclosure and short sales. She leads her real estate team with her business partner and husband, Gabe. Janet is also mother to her son, Tony. She enjoys driving on her Harley, traveling, decorating, organizing, and being a hockey goalie mom in Wisconsin. She wants to write a book one day and thought writing in this book was a great way to start. Her story faces both loss and gain and she wanted to share one example of how impactful and rewarding her real estate career has been. Visit* **www.ruffoloteam.kw.com** *for more information.*

DEBRA'S STORY

Janet Ruffolo

◆　◆　◆

I *thought it was about a house….*

My phone rang with a short sale call in August of 2016. A woman named Debra Peterson was calling because she received a letter from us that we send out to homeowners who are facing foreclosure. We spoke for a bit about her house and how I could help her avoid foreclosure by hiring me as her realtor to sell it through a short sale. I explained how my husband Gabe had a short sale team and we had been working together in this business for three years. We would not charge her anything to work with us and we would be there to help her every step of the way from start to finish. Then, I told her I would email her the necessary bank paperwork to get this process started.

A few *months* passed. I had reached out and left messages for her several times. She finally called me back and said she was working on completing the paperwork. She wanted to meet me at my office on October 25th to get all of her paperwork to me, so I scheduled an appointment for her to stop by.

Debra came in up the green handicap ramp of my office for her appointment. We were renting a small brick house that was converted to an office. She pushed her walker, which also had a seat on it. Debra looked older with short gray hair, piercing brown eyes, and she was thin and frail. She proceeded to get me her completed paperwork as she lifted the seat of her walker. It looked as if she had everything she needed in the seat of the walker, from pens to glasses. She was soft spoken and friendly and I could tell her mind was sharp. I tried to assist her a few times and she would not accept my assistance. She told me that, since she was only fifty-nine years old, she could manage.

I thanked her for completing the paperwork so well and explained the next step was that I would need to come to her house to take pictures and have her sign the needed listing agreement and offer from an investor friend of mine. Debra seemed hesitant and said she would have some cleaning to do before I came by. I assured her that I would be looking at her house and not the items in it. We agreed I would stop by the following afternoon.

As I approached the house for our appointment that October day, I felt overwhelmed because I was quite busy with my own life. Being a mom, wife, business partner, and realtor was more than I could manage on most days. In business, it is said that being busy is a good problem to have. The issue I have with that statement is that it has the word "problem" in it. There were so many *problems* I had to address every day. Everywhere I turned there were more and with no relief, it seemed.

I parked on the street and went up to this two-story house that had two doors on the porch. I knocked on the first one closest to the stairs, hoping I was at the right one. I waited for a minute and then saw Debra coming to the door. She peered through the glass to make sure she saw who was knocking. As she opened the door slowly and partially, she apologized for the mess. She said she was going through things she no longer wanted and planned to get rid of them. I walked into a room that appeared, at first glance, to be filled with lots of *stuff.* There was a small path from the living room that led us through a dining area and into the kitchen. The kitchen table, where I asked if we could sit, was filled with bags of food. They were everywhere – on the floor, on the chairs; and there were also boxes and piles of papers. She seemed embarrassed as she tried to move them around so I would have room to sit. I assured her that it was fine, and we just needed to complete some paperwork. I thought to myself, *'she knew I was coming here today.'*

Debra and her cat, Sam.

Debra shared with me that she lived alone, except for her kitten Sam, who she got from her neighbor Darryl. She told me all about Sam and how happy he made her and how he helped her not feel so alone. She said she went to the grocery store and doctor appointments and even shoveled by herself. She got a bit choked up and told me that she had breast cancer and had surgery to remove one breast, but—while she was in surgery—they discovered that she had a second form of breast cancer and had to remove her other breast. She went into extreme detail about this and how she lost her job because of being sick.

Debra had worked all her life and work was all she really had that was good in her life. She was married once, but that ended in divorce and she never had any children. After her job let her go, she could not make her mortgage payments and was so depressed that she would be losing the house that she had bought in 1998. She explained how terrible her life was and that she didn't know what she was going to do. I showed sympathy and tried to give her reassurance. The best thing I could think to tell her was that she did not sign up for cancer. It was not her fault that she got it. She accepted my honesty and sincerity.

Debra kept sobbing as she told me story after story. I got wrapped up in it for a while, but was also aware of why I was there. I needed to help this woman sell her house to the bank as a short sale. This meant she owed more to the bank than what the house was worth to sell. The bank would forgive her of the balance due because she qualified for a short sale, due to the hardship reason of having cancer.

The kitchen had a leak in its flat roof. The damage had gotten so large that parts of the ceiling were falling. She had no money for these repairs or anything else I might find.

◆　◆　◆

Eventually, I excused myself to walk around her house and take a few pictures of each room. I had to do this for my listing and to determine the condition of the entire home. I had done this many times before at lots of houses. It was challenging to even *see* Debra's house, though.

Each room was filled with *stuff*.

She got up to show me the jewelry she made and all the supplies she had to make her jewelry with. She loved to sew and told me the five cabinets in her dining room area were all filled with fabric. She seemed to lighten up as she talked about her sewing and making jewelry.

I went down into the basement that had steep stairs with no railings, a low ceiling, again boxes . . . everywhere, most of them empty, and a *new* washer and dryer. Debra said she was not allowed to go down there to do her own laundry per her doctor's orders.

Upstairs were two bedrooms and a half bath that was the size of a closet. Her bed looked like a large nest, as blankets and pillows were formed in a small spot on the right side of the bed where she could sleep.

Trying hard to focus on getting through the house, taking pictures, and making sure I had her sign everything I needed, I felt the need to get out of there. Looking at my watch, I had been there for two and a half hours and it was now dark out. I excused myself and told her I needed to go to get home to my family. She seemed to understand and was grateful for the time we had shared together.

As I walked outside, it was not just dark, but cold. I started my car and called my husband Gabe to let him know I was leaving her house and coming home. I started explaining to him all I had heard and I began to choke up. I told him I needed to go and could not talk about this right now. I hung up the phone and just started to cry; I burst into tears. My mind was trying to process all of it and my heart hurt. I sat in my cold car, shut off my mind from any thought and just wept. I didn't understand why I was crying so much, but I didn't feel the need to know why.

Typically, I do not cross the boundary line with my clients from professional to personal.

Debra was different.

Debra welcomed me into her life to be her friend. I learned her mom had died eight years previously and, since then, she'd lost contact with her three brothers who lived in Texas and Utah. She had not even told any of them that she had cancer and did not want them to know.

Our relationship developed as I continued to help her sell her house and I took her to doctor appointments that required the type of testing from which she could not drive herself home. Debra found a low-income apartment she wanted to move into. I started going to her house to help her downsize and get rid of her excess items. I soon was made aware that she was a hoarder and had an emotional tie to *things*. She had so much food . . . and most of it was expired. There were over thirty boxes of cake mix, five grocery bags filled with instant mashed potato packets, twenty jars of peanut butter, tons of juice bottles, bags of candy, and more. In the basement alone, I counted over thirty jugs of laundry detergent and an overabundance of shampoo, conditioner, and toothpaste.

Excess was everywhere, but Debra did not see it like this.

She said she needed this and that. She offered to give me some items here and there for my help. But, she usually followed these offers up with the comment, "just don't take it all." There is no way humanly possible that one single person could consume the amount of food and products she owned. I also thought about all the money she spent to keep herself surrounded with them.

It didn't stop at food and consumables; she also had enough fabric, beads, and jewelry supplies to have her own store. The problem was she was too sick to use most of it. She said she had not sewn in over three years. She did make me some special jewelry pieces that I will cherish forever.

Debra called me her angel. She said I was sent by God to help her. And help her, I did. I took *six vans full of stuff* to Goodwill. I started doing laundry for her, including her bedding, sheets, and towels. It was sad to think of how long it had been since her laundry was done since she could not go in the basement to do it. She was so excited to have clean bedding and I was happy to do it. It was the simple things in life that I took for granted. Never did I realize how someone could live without them.

◆ ◆ ◆

Debra needed to keep going to chemotherapy treatments for her cancer. I was never sure if she had or still had cancer. Was it gone? She said it was gone, but then why did she need to keep going to chemotherapy? I saw her port at one appointment, which is used to put the chemotherapy medicine in and the place from which blood was drawn. She thought I would be skittish to see it. I was . . . a little . . . but kept it all inside.

She developed chronic diarrhea. I took her for testing multiple times and they could never find out what was wrong. The doctors suspected it was a side effect from her gastric bypass surgery from sixteen years ago. She used to be heavy in her younger years and decided to have this done, never thinking of the long-term complications it could cause. She was unable to process most food and keep it in her system, which caused her to start losing weight. She was worried because she was getting too skinny.

Debra ended up in the hospital a short time after these complications. I went to visit her and she would vomit for hours on end. We talked about a lot of things as I sat with her. She asked me if I would take her beloved cat Sam if she ever died. I agreed to this and knew how special he was to her. He was life for her, and he kept her going, and was a good snuggle buddy as she slept a lot. It was hard to see her like this, but I wanted to be there. I also spoke with her about my becoming her medical or financial power of attorney. She had about $24,000 in her savings account. This was more money than almost all of my short sale clients typical have, but it was all she had from her entire life of working hard. I could not be power of attorney for both, even though—by this time—she trusted me with everything. She designated me medically with the hospital. This allowed me to get updates and information about her illness.

Debra introduced me to all the nurses as her *special friend* . . . when I was just her *realtor*.

In the hospital, they put her on TPN (Total Parenteral Nutrition) which was basically a feeding tube. It gave her body the calories, fluid, and nutrition she needed to stay alive. She had to be hooked up to this feeding machine for about twenty hours per day after she got out of the hospital. This lasted for a few weeks and she was eventually able to wean down on the time needed and then, finally, off it. Once off, she was still limited to a bland diet of mostly liquid-like foods. She got very frustrated and would even say, "what's the point of living if I can't even eat or enjoy food."

It was hard to do much for or with her because mostly everything involves food. Events, holidays, the quality time we look forward to, cooking, and baking – all involved food. I couldn't pick her up and take her out to eat. I invited her to holidays and she declined because she couldn't eat and didn't want to sit around and watch everyone else eat. I wanted to take her to church but she was worried she would make a mess by not making it to the bathroom on-time. She lived in adult diapers and complained that she was going through so many of them and they were costing her lots of money to buy. It was hard to process all these events, visits, and the time I was giving to help her.

Eventually, we got Debra moved over into her apartment. We had a church group of nine men come over to help her physically move one Saturday. We rented a truck so we could get everything in a few trips. We were not ready or packed enough for all this help. It was chaotic as I tried to coordinate all that the guys needed to do and keep an eye on Debra at the same time, who was still connected to her TPN. I made the decision to donate most of her excess food that was still good to a local food shelter. There was more than a truck load. I knew most of her stuff would not fit into her one-bedroom, small apartment. Luckily, the new place had a storage compartment that we were able to load up to the top with seven big boxes of fabric. She left most of her furniture at the house. She bought a new bedroom set and made sure all five of her fabric cabinets "fit" into her living space. She had two office desks, each with a chair. One was with her computer that she used to watch movies on (since she had no tv), look for recipes, and shop for *more* jewelry. The other desk had her two sewing machines on it and jewelry supplies all around it.

Debra was moved in and it seemed overwhelming to get her unpacked and settled in. She had just enough space . . . *for her stuff.* We talked of times we would get together to make chili and bake cookies and cake. She was excited to sew again and make her jewelry. I knew it was only a matter of time before she realized most of her food was gone. She called me one day and yelled at me because now she had nothing to eat and would have to go out and buy all new food again. It was the right decision that I had to make, so I just bit my tongue, listened, and apologized for the mix-up.

The short sale process seemed to be moving along very slowly, especially since I listed her house for sale on October 27th, 2016 for $24,900. We had an offer at the amount the bank wanted, but they still did not get the short sale approved. We had a sheriff sale date come up, when the house would be available for public auction for the bank to be able to recoup its money. We tried our hardest to stop it. We did so through lots of calls, time, and having Debra involved with them. I worried, too. After all this time and effort, the end of the story could not be that her house got sold at a sheriff sale. This wouldn't be fair and what kind of realtor would I be? I even called the short sale lender and pleaded with them to approve this short sale so we could close on it before she died! I explained how she had cancer and was still very sick.

As the next fall approached and the air became crisp and cold, it seemed like hard and busy times were ahead. This short sale had to get done, so we could end the chapter of selling her house. It had been a year already. Debra was getting anxious for the end, too, and wanted to sell her remaining furniture in the house. I volunteered to go with her after her doctor's appointment one day to take pictures and put the furniture in selling groups on Facebook. It was time consuming, but I knew it would all be over soon. Debra wanted me to put her phone number on the posts and assured me she would take the calls. I started getting comments that she was not calling them back after they had called multiple times. I tried calling her to talk about how this should be handled. She was not responding to my calls in a timely manner, either. I decided to run a sale one day for a few hours and she agreed to sit in her house for the sale. Only one person showed up. I was running out of options . . . and time. I hated when it seemed like a burden for me to help her with all of the details. This was way beyond the duty of a realtor. I was aware of this and chose to keep helping as her friend. I brought her a wooden plaque in the hospital that said:

"Friends become our chosen Family."

When I spoke with Debra, she said she was sleeping most of the day and awake all night, and therefore she had not been returning my calls. I wanted to stop by and see her but knew that her cat Sam had fleas the last few times I was there, so I had to keep my visits short. Thanksgiving came and went. I wanted to invite her with my family but knew she wouldn't have come because she was still not eating regular food. I left her a few messages after Thanksgiving to see how she was doing and to then let her know that she was in my thought and prayers. Days passed and she did not return any of my calls. I was starting to get concerned. She had done this another time and I explained to her that she needed to always get back to me after I call, so I would know she was ok. I worried about her being alone most of the time. It was good that she lived in an apartment building with lots of neighbors.

Living in a three-story apartment building was a big adjustment for her. She now had lots of people her age all around her. She made friends with a few ladies that lived on the first floor with her. They had cats and some had dogs too. It was a pretty social place from what I could see each time I came to pick her up and drop her off for her doctor's appointment and tests. I even met these ladies when Debra introduced them to me. Terry was one of them who had a key to Debra's place and kept an eye on Sam when she was in the hospital. Debra liked the inside of her place and Sam seemed happy there, too. It was less space for her to take care of and clean and she liked that everything was on one level.

I did notice that, each time I went to Debra's apartment, she would have more stuff – from boxes stacked, to more bags of excessive food, to bottles of soda. It was hard for me to make mention of this to her, but when she would complain and cry over the phone with me that she would not be able to afford to pay for all the new medicines that the doctors wanted her to start taking, I had to say something. I would gently mention that she then needed to watch what she was spending online for jewelry making beads, supplies, and food. She knew she had a problem buying more jewelry stuff than she needed and that it got expensive. I believe Debra was a hoarder of food, fabric, jewelry beads, jewelry-making supplies, and health care products . . . things of sustenance, beauty, and wellness that she didn't have in her life, anymore. I am not sure how someone can justify buying so much of one item that they will never possibly be able to use in their own lifetime. The very definition of hoarding, though, *is* to stockpile. It was a sense of security for her to surround herself with all this *stuff*. At one point, I had to do research on hoarding, the emotional side of it, and how I could learn to help her in the best way, both physically and emotionally. I even watched a few episodes of the reality show, *Hoarders*, but watched it in a different way, not in disgust at these sad people, but to educate myself.

◆ ◆ ◆

It was Friday, December 1st. I had not heard back from Debra after the few messages I'd left for her on the phone, so I decided to send her a little note. It read: "Debra, I hope this note finds you well. I have not heard back from you after my calls and wanted to make sure you were ok. I will stop by to see you in a few days, too." I went about my day and went to check on an empty house of mine that I was just about to get listed when I received the call.

"This is the apartment manager, Chris, calling about Debra Peterson. We found her in her apartment where she had passed away a few days ago. She had you down as her emergency point of contact and that you would take her cat Sam if something happened to her," he said.

I had a bad feeling that something had happened to her and that was why she was not calling me back. I don't remember a lot of details about that call other than I was in shock and about to face a bad reality. I sat down on the stairs of the vacant house and was still. I needed to go pick up my new cat Sam from Debra's apartment building lobby. (Oh, and he had fleas, so I would need to take him to a vet to get the proper flea medicine and shot if needed.) Chris said he was in a borrowed cage and was doing ok but seemed to be a bit shaken up. He'd found several bags of food and litter in her apartment that I could have. Apparently, the mailman mentioned to a neighbor that her mail had been stacking and a few neighbors had also heard Sam meowing repeatedly over the last few days. The manager decided to go check on her and that's when they found her.

I called my husband Gabe to tell him. I got a few words out and then the crying poured out as the burst of reality just hit me. He couldn't understand what I was saying until I let it out and then was able to compose my words. I was mostly concerned about Sam. I would need to get a pet carrier and go pick him up. I was so upset and happy at the same time. Upset I lost a dear friend and happy I would have a new cat, Debra's cat, to love, take into my home, and care for him as Debra did.

A sea of questions crashed like waves in my head.

'What happened to her? How long was she dead for before she was found? What was Sam doing? Did he have enough food to eat? When was the last time I even saw her? How did we say goodbye . . . because that was our last goodbye. How was I supposed to know that was the last time I would see her? What would happen from here and what about all of her stuff?' There were so many unknowns.

As I approached her apartment lobby entrance, I was uneasy. I walked in and the manager, Chris, met me with a big hug and said he was sorry. The city coroner also met me and gave me his card. He explained that it was best for me not to see her because it was bad. They would contact her family. I already decided that I would not emotionally be able to handle going into her apartment and I never did. At this point, I was "just" her realtor, but was the one person who had the most information about her. With a short sale, she had to provide me with her entire identity, and I also had authority to receive her medical information.

As I talked to these men, I watched Sam, who was curled up and trembling in one small corner of a large, hard, dog cage. I was painfully waiting to get Sam from that cage. As soon as I was alone, I took him out, held him, and just cried. He shook and meowed at first and then calmed down. I took in every ounce of emotion I was feeling and envisioned the trauma this poor cat had gone through. It was mixed emotions of loss and gain to me, along with a flood of others.

I remembered my son Tony asking if we could get a cat a few months ago and I said no because we knew we would get Debra's cat Sam someday. Today was that day. It felt good to hold my promise to a client that had become such a close and *special friend* to me. It was somehow easier to grieve the loss of her by holding, caring for, and bringing this special life into our home and family.

On November 6th 2014, nearly two years before meeting Debra, I had let my precious cat Tasha outside and she never came back. How I missed her and mourned her. God had found a special way to replace the loss of my cat Tasha with a special cat Sam. I let this all sink into my heart.

Debra was cremated and put in the wall of a local cemetery. A number was assigned to her place on the wall. Her two brothers ended up coming to go through her apartment and tie up loose ends. They never claimed her body . . . or the bill from the city that went along with it. I was devastated when I was made aware of this when I spoke with the coroner. Eventually, her brother did claim her and took care of the bill. They needed to do so to get a death certificate, go through probate . . . and be able to have her money released to them.

There was never a memorial service held for Debra.

We never were able to sell her house as a short sale.

After Debra died, her home was foreclosed on and sold at a sheriff sale on April 18th (one day before my birthday) of 2018 to an investor who was also an agent.

As a real estate transaction, I never made one penny from this house; in fact . . . I had *failed* to sell it at all.

I gained a special friend who I was able to help, who taught me so much, and who gave me the gift of her cat, Sam. Although she is gone, she will always be remembered in my heart and every time I look at Sam. As I walked in the house that first brought us together, shortly after she died, it hit me that *it was never about a house....*

Written in Honor of my special friend, Debra Lynn Peterson, March 14, 1956 – December 1, 2017.

◆　◆　◆

"Faith is moving without

knowing."

~ Hebrews 11:8 (Paraphrase)

Dave Bruno has been a Realtor since 2002. He is also a Quotologist and, in 1990, turned a practice of saving quotations into a motivation business after nearly dying in an auto accident which led to bankruptcy and home foreclosure. He got the idea after learning of a miraculous sequence of events that saved his life. Dave has written two quote books, "Never Give Up - Empowering Thoughts for Challenging Times" and "Real Estate Drama - Winning the Head Games." Dave uses quotations in his Real Estate marketing and branding. Dave lives with Marlene, his wife of thirty-seven years, near their three grown sons and two granddaughters.

SPREAD A LITTLE SUNSHINE

Dave Bruno

◆ ◆ ◆

"In the middle of every difficulty lies opportunity."
~Albert Einstein

'*I can't breathe! I can't breathe!*' I screamed inside my head as my lungs collapsed. '*Oh my God, I'm going to die. What about my wife and three sons-I can't leave them? This isn't the way its supposed to end.*'

My wife Marlene was told I was resuscitated three times and she should prepare for the worst. When I opened my eyes the next day, Marlene was peering down at me with a puppy dog look and the only things I remember her saying were, "I love you," and, "Just concentrate on getting better."

She said nothing about the details of the car accident which had shattered my body – a body that was now on life support. Most of my ribs were fractured or broken, my heart was bruised, my spleen was ruptured and removed, a third of my shredded liver was taken out, and I had massive internal bleeding and numerous other injuries. A medical team, along with fourteen tubes, needles, and catheters, as well as a respirator were keeping me alive . . . and I didn't even know how I got here.

During the next three days, I drifted in and out of consciousness. I knew my life was hanging in the balance. Fear, indescribable pain, and a morphine drip combined to make my imagination run wild. I began to believe that I wasn't being told all of the details of the accident because I had injured or killed someone and Marlene wasn't telling me because she knew that it would be too much for me to handle while I was trying to survive.

Nobody knew my heart was constantly pounding hard for fear of tragic news. I was freaking out believing I had hurt or killed someone.

The worst part was that I had been drinking.

Everything was my fault.

How could I have been so negligent?

I begged God over and over to change time or do whatever He had to do to ensure that no one else was harmed.

Over those three days, my thoughts tortured me. I couldn't ask any questions because I was on a respirator. It finally dawned on me to motion for something to write with.

"Was there anyone else in the accident?" I scribbled in a notebook.

Marlene gave me this puzzled look and said, "No, you were alone."

I instantly felt the weight of the world being lifted off my chest as my heart leapt for joy! My thoughts immediately shifted from panic and terror to immense gratitude and joy. All my vital signs improved instantly and dramatically. My heart, which had been racing for three days at 220 beats per minute (near maximum) plunged to eighty beats per minute within an hour. The medical staff was stunned with the swiftness that my condition improved. One moment, my thoughts were conspiring to kill me and now my thoughts were contributing in healing me.

Our thoughts are so powerful!

"Coincidence is God's way of remaining anonymous."
~Albert Einstein

Eventually, I was told how events unfolded....

At 1:30 am on a cold winter night, I crashed my car into a brick wall on a dark country road. At the moment I crashed, there just *happened to be* an ambulance less than a mile away driving toward me. They miraculously arrived at the scene of the accident within minutes of my crash. I was found hanging out of the side of the passenger door and I was quickly loaded into the ambulance. They sped off to a hospital which just *happened to be* only a mile away . . . and it just *happened to be* a regional trauma center.

If I would have been on the road a minute longer, or would have taken another minute to get to the hospital, I would have bled to death because of my burst spleen, or suffocated because of my collapsed lungs. This string of coincidences that *"just happened to be"* was Divine Intervention stepping in and taking charge during my brush with death.

It was not my time.

Then a very strange thing happened; a voice in my head said, *'Do something with the quotes.'* The message was so intense that it temporarily distracted me from the pain, but I had no idea what the voice meant. 'Do what? With what quotes?' The quotes that came to mind were quotes and sayings that I had written down on loose pieces of paper, post it notes, notecards, napkins, receipts, and paper bags and put into a box that I kept next to my desk. When I considered the coincidences that enabled me to be alive, I took it as a directive to find out what "Do something with the quotes" meant. At that moment I committed to doing whatever it took to find out. I was on a mission.

My appreciation and love of quotes was kindled growing up in a home where quotes, humorous sayings, axioms, proverbs, and psalms reigned. My mom and dad had a comeback quote or quip for any and all situations. My mom would write down quotes and, to encourage us, she would tape them to the refrigerator, bathroom mirror, or on the walls of my dad's home office.

Many times I heard my mom say "I just try to spread a little sunshine." Sharing quotes was one way she did it.

Just like my mom, I became a ravenous collector of inspirational quotes and sayings. When the right words gave me an "A-HA! Moment," I would write them down and they would end up on my wall, in my wallet, or somewhere I would see them often enough to keep me motivated. When and if a quote was replaced by a newer inspiration, the original words would be saved in my box of keepers.

"See things as you would have them instead of as they are."
~Robert Collier

The day after I learned the details of my accident, a medical team visited me and told me that it could be six to nine months before I would start to return to normal; I was unsure what they meant by "normal." I thought, *'Bullshit. Before the accident I was in great shape and I'm going get back to working out and prove them wrong.'*

I requested a physical therapist. I couldn't yet move my legs and it took a week of rehab before I could take my first step. And that's how I got better . . . step by step. As a believer in the power of visualization, I began trying to picture myself soaking up the sun and enjoying the view as I ran along beautiful, vast, and powerful Lake Michigan. I imagined myself cross country skiing through the moguls and plains of Kettle Moraine Forest on my favorite trail. I tried my best to forget about the pain and concentrate on the potential. I changed my thinking from thoughts of despair to thoughts of vitality.

I was told it would be at least two months until I would go home. Three weeks later, I returned home to continue my recovery and reorganize my life. Most of my days were spent in bed reading motivational books and adding to my box of quotes. I pushed myself while exercising each day and I continued to improve physically and mentally.

I thought, *'I have my life. I have my family, and no one else was in the accident.'* I felt like I was the luckiest guy on the planet. I believed my life was turning around, because the last year had been a tough one.

Dave and his family.

◆　◆　◆

In addition to the accident I'd been in, my mom died from lung cancer. Our son Michael almost died at birth from a Strep B infection; he was confined to an incubator for ten days. During his first two months of life, he slept in our bedroom with the LED lights on an apnea monitor blinking all night. I lost my job as a sales manager. My accident had occurred just two days before I was to start a new career selling advertising, an opportunity that was now gone, because I was unable to work. Meanwhile, our cash reserves were getting dangerously low.

Things continued to get worse.

I learned our temporary insurance coverage was next to worthless considering the astronomical hospital bills that we would soon be facing. I totaled one car in the accident and our other car was repossessed. I had no income and I was physically unable to work. After a long struggle trying to keep up with medical bills and battling with creditors, we declared bankruptcy.

It seemed that no matter how bad things got, I could always find a silver lining. All of my hard work payed me a big reward just four months to the day after the accident. I completed a three-mile run sponsored by the hospital where I almost died, (and where good and well-meaning doctors told me "Six to nine months until you begin to feel normal.")

We shouldn't let limitations expressed by others become the expectations we have for ourselves. We choose our limitations and possibilities. I was broke but I still felt totally empowered!

Foreclosure was next.

I will always vividly remember the day we lost our home and had to move to a crowded apartment. I was feeling pretty bummed out. I had taken a job in advertising to make ends meet and, after my sales appointments for the day were over, I returned to my office.

The receptionist peered at me with a peculiar look on her face and said, "Dave, Waukesha Memorial Hospital called and your wife and sons were in an accident with a school bus. They wouldn't say how they were doing. They just said that you should get there as soon as you can."

I FELT PANIC!

That's the same kind of message Marlene received when I had my accident . . . when they weren't sure if I would survive!

I thought, *'This is impossible. We are losing our home today because of my car accident, and today my entire family has just been in another accident. Help me.'*

I couldn't take anymore. Life was too heavy. I dropped my briefcase and began crying in front of fifty sets of eyes, fearing that my wife or my sons were killed.

Everything seemed surreal when I arrived at the hospital. There were camera crews from two local TV stations at the emergency entrance. Flashing lights and people scurrying all around only added to my confusion.

I was led down a hallway.

It felt like I was walking uphill.

The floor was angled toward the ceiling.

When I got to their room, Marlene had her arm in a sling and the boys had a few black eyes. *But they were okay.* No one was hurt in the school bus that ran a red light and got knocked on its side when it hit our car .

"Thank you, God!" For the second time in an hour, I dropped to my knees sobbing, but this time I was filled with gratitude.

◆   ◆   ◆

Another challenge greeted us the day Marlene called me in hysterics to tell me that the IRS just seized the last $90.00 we had in our checking account and we didn't have enough money to pay the rent. What I did next nearly broke me. I went to the bank and withdrew $1000 from my son's paper route account in order to pay the rent and put some food on the table.

I was humiliated and devastated . . . but I was not defeated.

I believed my life had been spared for a reason and that I would find out what "Do something with the quotes" meant. I just had to be patient.

> *"It's not whether you get knocked down, it's whether you get up!"*
> *~Vince Lombardi*

Soon things did begin improving. My new career in advertising was really beginning to pick up steam. I believed learning about and selling advertising would prove valuable in helping me discover more about printing, advertising, and marketing. Then, my A-HA! moment would signal the beginning of a business opportunity that would help me to . . . "Do something with the quotes." When I wasn't working, I continued researching, gathering, and organizing quotes.

Oftentimes, customers would say something to the effect of, *'I've got important team building and leadership events coming up and I don't have a lot of money to spend. Do you have any ideas for something cheap that doesn't look like junk, and has some meaning to it that will make attendees want to keep it?'* That's a very tall order. I knew that I would have a winner when I came up with a vehicle incorporating my quotes that would do those things.

I was working on a membership program with one of my customers and they wanted to print a membership card. CLICK. *'That's it! That's the answer. I'll print the quotes on credit cards and create a product line of motivational pocket cards. That was so obvious. Why did it take me four years to figure this jigsaw puzzle out?'*

When I came home after work, I was so fired up thinking I had finally discovered the meaning of "Do something with the quotes."

I needed to come up with a design. I walked past the TV while a commercial for MasterCard Gold Card was on. Immediately it came to me: I would print my inspiring quotes on gold credit card stock and call it "The Success Gold Card." They would be high class, low cost, and people would love them.

It took me four years of obsession to find my treasure and in only four hours for all of the pieces of the puzzle to come together. That's how life works sometimes.

The more I organized and rearranged my quotes, the more I realized I was creating something very special and unique. There were limitless quote books, and lists of quotes available. Sometimes one quote said the same thing or something very similar as the next quote on the list. I was grouping quotes into what I called "Quote Vignettes." These Quote Vignettes linked carefully selected quotes and truisms to work in concert with one another, inducing the reader to concentrate on a life situation, an idea, a mindset, or an attitude. Unlike generic quote lists, a Quote Vignette includes a series of quotes carefully selected and arranged to work together. They build on one another to help you reflect on your life and circumstances from a positive perspective. Most importantly, each quote stands on its own as a powerful, inspirational message. I speak about the Quote Vignettes passionately because they brought passion back to my life.

"Take time to deliberate; but when the time for action arrives, stop thinking and go in."
~Andrew Jackson

I was ready to take a leap of faith. My satirical self decided to start my quote business on April Fool's Day 1990 with no money, no customers, no product, bad credit, and against everyone's advice . . . but with a great idea. Because I didn't have money to pay a printer to print my Gold Cards I taught myself how to screen print. I rented a hell hole of a shop in a tough neighborhood for $50.00 month. My first order was a card titled "Motivation" for a great friend of mine who was a sales manager. For the sales meeting, he ordered seven cards with the Nabisco logo on them and used the quotes to lead the discussion. I grossed $14.00 in sales at $2.00 a card. With set-up charges it cost me $55.00 to print the order. In other words, I lost $41, but I was on my way. I printed extra cards for samples. Now I could demonstrate how an International Company used my product. More orders began to follow.

My first-year sales were $9,000. Three years later I was making significantly more money than I ever had in my life. In twelve years, I sold more than two million Success Gold Cards in over 500 retail stores, as well as purchased by most of the Fortune 500 companies. I customized cards for hundreds of companies and organizations that were given to thousands of people including two United States Presidents. I received a phone call from a family member at the request of President George H.W. Bush for a card I created and sent to soldiers in Iraq. Another customized Gold Card was given to President Clinton at a meeting he attended. But my all-time favorite transaction occurred when I donated 400 Gold Cards of quotes from Mother Teresa. They were given to attendees from all over the world at a United Nations meeting while Mother Teresa was being eulogized.

Wow, was I blessed!

Speaking opportunities began presenting themselves after local newspapers published articles about my car accident and our family business. The Associated Press picked it up we were again interviewed, this time for national syndication. My story also appeared in a popular magazine at the time, Success Magazine's Great Comeback issue . . . which brought in more business. It seemed that everything was going my way. We had nicely transitioned from our bankruptcy and foreclosure to living in a nice, four-bedroom home in a great neighborhood. We had two new cars, no debt, and a modest amount of money in the bank. We weren't rich but we were able to breathe easily for the first time in seven years.

For the next four years, business kept humming along, but the winds of change began blowing again. My biggest customer sold Success Gold Cards in stores across the country and accounted for forty percent of my sales. I received a verbal purchase order and I printed their largest order ever. A written purchase order was to follow. This was not the first time we had done this so I had no cause for concern.

I didn't foresee that the entire purchasing department was going to be replaced and a new buyer would tell me my Gold Cards were no longer going to be sold, purchase orders not in writing would not be honored, and they would not be accepting or paying for the inventory I had printed especially for them. I had invested most of my available cash to print this order. Having it cancelled was a severe blow, not only because I had just lost my biggest customer, but now I had too much inventory and cash flow problems. Shortly after this, my second largest retail customer began closing stores and I took another substantial hit. I lost seventy percent of my business from my two largest customers in the blink of an eye.

Then . . . 9/11.

It was a tragic day for tragic and painful reasons, we all know. For my business, though—as was the case for many professionals around the country—it was the beginning of the end. Sales were heavily influenced by corporate training. Travel budgets were slashed. Orders for "extras" like my Gold Cards came to a standstill. It had taken me fifteen years to get to a successful point after hearing "Do something with the quotes," and—within a few months—I had gone from feast to famine.

One day, Marlene came to me with a sad look on her face and very softly said, "Dave, you have to find a job. We're out of money." My heart ached – she was right.

"When one door closes, another opens; but we often look so long and so regretfully upon the closed door that we do not see the one which has opened for us."
~Alexander Graham Bell

About a week after I had my conversation with Marlene, I drove past a For Sale sign and thought, *'I should sell real estate. Actually, I bet I could sell a lot of real estate. I know so many people. Wait. What the heck am I thinking? I don't find anything appealing about selling real estate. I don't know anything about, nor am I interested in houses, and I don't want to work nights and weekends.'*

Marlene and my four sisters laughed when I told them I was thinking of starting a real estate career and I didn't blame them. In fact, I laughed along with them. I thought window treatments were the plastic you put over your windows to keep the heat in. I didn't even know the difference between a ranch and a cape cod. I was uniquely *un*qualified to sell real estate, but I couldn't shake the thought of the potential for selling homes. I had built a huge network in a small community where I lived most of my life, and from which I graduated high school thirty-two years earlier. I was constantly volunteering at our schools, church, and community events. Plus, fifteen years of coaching youth sports had put me in touch with so many families.

I knew a lot of people.

Timing is Everything. The timing to get into real estate was perfect. Residential real estate was on fire in 2001. If you could fog a mirror, you could sell some homes. If you were good and knew a lot of people, you could sell a lot of homes. If you were a guy looking for work after closing his company, you could sell a lot of homes. My friends were becoming empty nesters and downsizing. Their parents were selling their homes and moving to senior living and condos, and soon my kids and their friends would be buying houses. I couldn't have started at a better time. I was ready for this.

Letting go of my Gold Card business was both painful and satisfying at the same time. It was an incredible twelve-year year run. Not only did I find out what "Do Something with the quotes" meant (and I actually did do something with the quotes), but now it was time to dust myself off and move forward in a new direction. The pain of walking away from the business that I loved was eased when I began a successful career selling real estate.

I became a realtor July 3, 2002.

It was my 50th birthday, during the hottest home selling market ever. Financially we felt rescued. Whew!

I started to think my mission to do something with the quotes had been completed and a chapter in my life was being closed, however, I was mistaken. I soon began incorporating my love of quotes into my real estate advertising and marketing. Twelve years of selling quotes convinced me that people love quotes and it was a great way of separating myself from other realtors. When realtors advertise, oftentimes it seems they are talking about themselves. By using quotes in my advertising I gave people something that would give them a smile, a warm feeling, or encouragement. That would help them remember and associate me with a positive impression.

My first day as a realtor, I did a mailing announcing I had become a realtor to my sphere of influence and I included a Success Gold Card on "attitude." I was pleased that I received several phone calls thanking me for the card. Shorty after the mailing, I did my first print advertising with quotes and it paid big dividends. I advertised in my community's High School Football Program. I placed business card-sized ads with motivational quotes throughout the entire section of the program that had individual student-athlete photos (viewed mostly by the parents). People came up and talked to me throughout the entire game: "I love your ads." Several people also made comments about the mailing I had just done "I love that card with the quotes you sent in the mail." That one-night jump started my real estate business and I was off to the races. Quotes worked and were there for me again. I used them in my branding, advertising, newsletters, merchandising, and communications.

I still had one big quote creation on my bucket list. I never completed the quote book I was writing when my business collapsed. In 2009, I went to work to write and publish my first quote book, *Never Give Up-Empowering Thoughts for Challenging Times*. In addition to book sales, it has served me well as a marketing piece to clients and realtors, but mainly . . . I checked it off my bucket list. It's loaded with many of my favorite quotes and it sits on my desk, ready to be opened the next time I need a dose of inspiration.

When I started real estate, I began building a new collection of quotes that I found helpful in dealing with real estate issues. In 2017 I wrote and published my second quote book, *Real Estate Drama-Winning the Head Games*.

*Dave's books can be purchased at **quotelovers.com**.*

I like to say it took me fifteen years to write my second book because that's how long it took me to gather and organize the quotes. I wrote the book to help realtors who experience the same challenges I did, the ups and downs of the real estate market, dealing with rejection, being persistent, working brutal schedules, and dealing with empathy for my clients when a real estate transaction goes bad. I also give the book as a closing gift to my co-brokes.

"People and circumstances come into our lives or A Reason, A Season, or a Lifetime."

Thirty-three years later, I am reminded of my accident every day. Pain from scar tissue and sore ribs take care of that. Battling guilt is also something I still deal with. After all, I was drinking the night of the accident. Some people won't respect me because of that and, quite frankly, I don't blame them. It was a wakeup call for me. But I still have to keep moving forward. I am proof that we can turn our big mistakes into huge triumphs.

Having the experience of thinking my life was over and getting a second chance is an advantage that very few people have. It has given me a deep appreciation for life and the realization that life, and each of life's seasons has time limits. This realization gives me a sense of urgency to get certain things done before it's too late. It also gives me a desire for balance and to let alone the things that really don't matter at the end of the day.

My love of quotes is part of my DNA. I will always be on a crusade to do the *next thing* with the quotes, even if it is only to keep myself inspired. There is tremendous power in our thoughts. Seeing and internalizing quotes and positive messages serve us well to encourage, inspire, and motivate us to overcome challenges. Challenges will always be part of life. My computer and office walls will always be covered with quotes to help me meet those challenges head on and it's a wonderful feeling knowing that inspiring and motivating messages that I have created for more than thirty years are all over the world helping others to meet their challenges.

> *"I just try to spread a little sunshine."*
> *~Mom*

"Don't aspire to be the best

ON the team, aspire to be

the best FOR the team."

~ *Unknown*

BUSINESS

◆　◆　◆

It's important in a business worth owning to function with honesty and integrity. You should embrace professionalism, proficiency, and be passionate about the business, while striving to provide an extraordinary client experience.

A business team worth pursuing should include a combination of unique talents and experiences, bringing value to the mission. Good team members are lifelong students who leverage their talents to become a fierce force to be reckoned with. Respect, inspire, serve, and hold one another accountable to performing at the highest level. Operate effectively and efficiently by aligning with proven systems and innovative technologies to become profitable

The reward is in achieving goals, providing an extraordinary client experience, giving back to the community, and serving one another.

◆　◆　◆

"The path of mastering

something is not only doing

the best you can, but also

the best it can be done."

~ Gary Keller

Real estate is **Julia Kellogg**'s second career. Having come from thirty plus years as a corporate executive, she utilizes her skillsets to nurture and guide her clients to successful outcomes, while building lifelong relationships along the way. What drives her is the opportunity to teach and mentor others. Julia a board member of several non-profit organizations and is actively involved in volunteering opportunities to help those in her community. She enjoys traveling the world and, when at home with her husband and three westies, she fills her time with knitting, cooking, or doing mixed media collage in her art studio. "I cannot do all the good that the world needs. But the world needs all the good that I can do." ~ Jana Stanfield

MY PURPOSEFUL LIFE

Julia Kellogg

◆ ◆ ◆

A s long as I can remember, I've wrestled and struggled with defining my purpose here on this earth. I've often asked myself, *'what am I here to accomplish and what legacy, if any, will I leave behind?'*

In my quest for answers I would find myself turning to my trusted resource for internal and spiritual guidance. I'm talking about Oprah Winfrey, of course! I would delve into every article or book I could get my hands on that addressed this very subject: finding one's purpose. The funny thing is that, although most articles were interesting reads, I could not find the *answer* I was looking for in a book, magazine article, or on her Super Soul Sunday series.

My search was to figure out this burning question inside of me and to uncover the truth of my existence. *'Am I doing what I was set upon this earth to do or am I just living out my time here?*

In my quest for the answer, little did I realize getting one is a journey unto itself – a journey that begins when we are children. Our own awareness and knowledge weave themselves into a tapestry of self-truths and values. These are pieces of who we become and, if we embrace the little bit of for which we are here, we discover, not one answer to my many questions, but a process to getting those answers. That process is what unveils itself over time.

My journey began as the youngest of three siblings growing up in a modest home in Oklahoma. After a long and drawn out divorce, my mother remarried and—at the age of three—my new father uprooted our entire family and moved us to Europe to start our new life. Leaving the United States took us away from a very long custody battle that had turned cruel and abusive towards my two siblings. Fortunately, I was too young to be a victim of the war between my biological parents. It wasn't until many years later that I understood our family move to Europe was an escape for my parents and a new start for all of us.

It was not glamorous to move to Europe as many friends and family thought, but merely out of necessity for our health and well-being. It was also not easy living in a foreign country. There were language barriers, cultural differences, and—although we never lacked for the basic necessities—finances were scarce. We lived close to an Army base, as my father worked with the military. To help ease the pressures of our living expenses, my mother went to work for the United States Government shortly after I started kindergarten.

Hanging with friends while living in Germany.

In our family, it was expected that we would earn a college degree. As a young girl I would fantasize where my adulthood would lead me. At first, I decided I wanted to be a ballet dancer. Ever since I'd had the opportunity to take a few classes that a family friend graciously provided, it had become a dream of mine. The first ballet instructor I had was Mrs. Smoak; she instilled confidence in me and the drive to not give up. Even if we were tired or had blisters on our feet, she would say at every practice or recital, "you've made a commitment to yourself and you need to follow through and do your best work."

Little did I realize then what an inspiration Mrs. Smoak would be to me. She would help to shape how I approached much of my life from that point on. I stayed with dance throughout high school and college, but realized I did not possess the talent required to be a professional dancer. I turned to my other passion . . . which was fashion.

I studied Fashion Merchandising and upon graduating with a degree, landed my first retail job as an Assistant Buyer for a company and I had the aspiration of travel. As the retail industry began to evolve with department store closings and acquisitions, I experienced several job changes. Fortunately, in the midst of those transitions, I found my way to Wisconsin. I began working for a then-small chain of stores by the name of Kohl's Department Stores. This little company was on the brink of its breakout and my timing was a Godsend for me in so many ways. When I joined the company in 1987, there were forty-one stores in operation throughout the upper Midwest. Within a bit over twenty years, Kohl's would became a national chain with over 1,100 stores . . . and growing.

In my career with Kohl's, I held a number of positions in the company that required extensive travel across the United States, Europe, and Asia. My travel aspirations had come true. In order to survive in a culture of excellence, I felt I constantly had to re-invent myself to stay on top of my game, both as a leader and a business woman. It was not enough to deliver on expectations, but *how* you delivered was just as important.

I discovered a passion for mentoring my team members as well as those who sought out my guidance. I was flattered, but also humbled by their trust. Watching others I'd helped excel in *their* careers made me proud, especially to see many of them move on to even greater things.

The years sped forward and the company continued to grow exponentially, but I began to question my own destiny. I had grown tired of having to re-inventing myself to fit in to a company culture that, though it fulfilled my passions of travel and fashion, did not align with my personal beliefs.

Throwing myself into the latest self-help or leadership book was how I thought I'd find my way again with Kohl's, but I continued to come up feeling empty and lost. I *loved* the people I worked with and, especially, my team. However, I was simply *burned out* and found I could not get behind the mission and values of the workplace for which I had so loved the actual work while I stood behind them, mentored within their structure, and fought for their importance over the years.

Fulfilling the *tasks* of my dreams was no longer enough for me. I was looking for something more; I couldn't put my finger on what it was, but I knew I had to move on. I felt I was internally suffocating. I dreaded Mondays and rejoiced on Fridays. That's when I knew it was time for me to go. The things that dissatisfied had grown larger than those that satisfied. It was a call away from discontentment.

What I knew of myself as I entered transition:

I was drawn to and had a desire for helping others.

I enjoyed volunteering for organizations I could support.

◆　◆　◆

Volunteering is a way of life!

The stars were aligned and, just a few days after leaving Kohl's, I contacted a dear friend who had, earlier in the year, tried to connect me with a few organizations. I had been too busy with my work at that time to engage. Over lunch, my friend shared several non-profit organizations, like the *Make-A-Wish Foundation* and *The Women's Center*. She supported those groups, believed I would, as well, and knew I could use my corporate experience to help. It was up to me to find the right fit . . . and I did!

Although both organizations have great missions, *The Women's Center* in Waukesha's county supporting safety, shelter, and support for victims of domestic violence, sexual assault, and trafficking of women and children was the one I connected with. I have been involved with their organization for over four years now and am constantly in awe of the heroic work this shelter does, day after day, educating and healing women and children from the physical and emotional scars of their abusers. They are truly saving lives, one at a time.

This special place I could now pour into touched my heart and spirit immediately. Maybe I was connected because my own mother had nowhere to turn in the late Fifties and early Sixties when she was suffering at the hands of her abuser, my biological father. If I could help make a difference through my time and resources, hopefully I would be impacting someone desperately in need. *The Women's Center* gave me an opportunity help support those in that desperate need. I felt an obligation to try and make a difference through spreading the word of this vital organization through my commitment of time and resources.

Once engaged in volunteering, I realized rather quickly that I needed something to further occupy my time. Through a friend's strong urging, I obtained my real estate license, and quickly realized how much I enjoyed learning something new. More importantly, I discovered the value that I could provide clients through both buying and selling real estate. I could help others move forward with their lives for various reasons, whether it be due to the needs of a growing family, the unfortunate loss of a spouse, or a job transfer, this new path really energized me and motivated me to greet every morning with anticipation of what the day would bring. The ability to help clients navigate these life changes brings me joy.

Both of my current vocations have also afforded me the freedom and flexibility to travel on trips for pleasure, as well as for important work. I have always loved to travel, as I find that discovering new countries and cultures continues to shape my thinking, my behavior, and my heart. It has opened my eyes to seeing things differently. Realizing your own lifestyle is often vastly different to the people, food, and surroundings right in front of you provides a worldview that allows me to recognize beauty and love in many forms. In most cases the language is different, but you can find a common ground through pointing, hand gestures, and a warm smile. Somehow you find yourself communicating and bridging cultural differences

◆   ◆   ◆

As I reflect on my life and my experiences, I recognize how I was shaped in my childhood with lessons in chosen adversity for our protection and working through the pain to feel the dance. In college, I learned that letting go of one dream opened the path to another. I discovered my love for mentoring in my first career and carried that, coupled with my passion for volunteering and supporting good causes to my second career. I've discovered the love of work can exist when you love what that work can do for others. And I've been blessed to absorb the cultural experiences that have broadened my world both literally and figuratively. All of these experiences have molded who I have become and more clearly defined my purpose. Although my journey hasn't ended, I've discovered I want my legacy to be about simply helping others achieve their goals in life.

For some, they must discover their purpose and then live their lives. For me, I have lived my life and – in it – discovered my purpose.

"What you get from

achieving your goals is not

as important as who you

become by achieving your

goals."

~ Zig Ziglar

Delisa Yaeger's passion for learning, serving, and sharing has supported clients, associates, friends, church, community, scouting, and family for more than thirty years. She nurtures personal and business relationships with a sense of humor, attention to detail, creative problem solving, and a tenacity to probe beyond first impressions. The culture of training, personal growth, and teamwork at Keller Williams supports her goal to serve even more clients with buying, selling, or investing dreams. Delisa and her husband Dave currently live in Waterford, Wisconsin with their teenage twin boys, Jon and Shawn, while children Lexi and Clayton, along with most of her extended family live in Central Illinois.

FOR THE BALANCE OF LIFE

Delisa Yaeger

W hat a way to start the new year!

Forty-five minutes into my initial physical therapy consultation, I realized and blurted out loud, "So, if I had come to you back in June, the three-minute procedure you are about to do, could have fixed this?"

She nodded with a knowing smile and I said, "Really, once again self-inflicted!"

Sure enough, after the three-minute procedure, which was uncomfortable, but not nearly as bad as I had imagined, the spinning, dizziness, brain fog, and lack of balance were gone. Hopeful, yet skeptical, I spent the next three days noticing the positions that no longer tipped me over. As my stability returned, so did my analytical and reflective mental gymnastics. *'Why was I so afraid of the procedure? What a waste of six months! How much did I miss?'*

The effects of Benign Paroxysmal Positional Vertigo (BPPV) pretty much sidelined my first summer as a Keller Williams real estate agent in 2018. That first day in June was the worst! Monday morning, the first day of the boys' summer vacation, I felt really lopsided walking down the stairs seeking coffee. Dave, my husband, had just left for work, so I sat down on the couch. That did not help, so I lay down on the floor. Even worse. Finally, I sat on the floor with my back against the couch, head straight up, and found *some* (not total) relief.

I was so dizzy and nauseous that every movement, no matter how slight, started the spinning all over again.

After about twenty minutes of stillness, my mind was racing: *'What's wrong with my balance? What caused the dizziness? How am I going to wake up the boys? Need to send thank you notes from yesterday's open house! Need to go to the hospital. Where's my phone? Crap . . . upstairs on the charger! Need to slow down!'*

I yelled for Shawn and Jonathan, my teenaged twins. One was upstairs sound asleep. The other, also sleeping, was in the soundproof basement; yelling did not work.

More racing thoughts: *'Where is the TV remote, I'll turn it up so loud it will wake one of them up. Okay, might work. Crap, the remote is on the side table, by the land line. If the TV does not work, I can call Dave at work.'*

For the next forty-five minutes, I would move a bit, let the spinning stop, move again, let the spinning stop, until I finally could reach the remote. The looking-up motion while reaching for the remote, initiated a severe puke response, which took even more time to subside. Finally, the TV was on max volume; still no response from either of the boys. *'I know, call his cell phone. Nope, straight to voice mail. Must be dead. Plan C, or is it D, call Dave at work.'*

When I finally got a response from a live human, it was nearly 9:30 A.M. Exhausted, freaked out, and fighting off the puke response, I attempted to explain to Dave what was wrong, what I was trying to do, and what he needed to do all at the same time. Fortunately, he is very accustomed to my frantic, jumbled, rapid-fire, circular communications. He was able to text one of our neighbors, with the garage code, to come wake up Shawn, while I was still trying to explain how long it took just to get to the phone.

Our hero neighbor calmly came into the house, checked to make sure I was okay, and then frightened my dead-to-the-world teenager upstairs.

"Shawn, Your Mom Needs you NOW," in a very stern voice, was exactly the solution I needed.

My neighbor also explained my symptoms were most likely vertigo and Shawn should take me to Urgent Care. It's not what I wanted to hear, even though I knew he was right. Now I needed to get up, get dressed, find my purse, and make sure the insurance card was in my wallet . . . all with the room spinning and the worst brain fog ever. Nothing compared to the thought of riding in the car, on winding back roads, with a teenager who had only been driving for three months, in a pickup truck, no less. *'I know, let's call the nurse hotline. Hopefully they will say, 'just stay home.''* No such luck.

The ride in the car was brutal for both of us. The more I grabbed the dash or door handle, the more anxious Shawn became, which made the curves even more pronounced. Once in the parking lot, it took a few minutes to slow down the spinning before I could walk. It was afternoon by the time I was checked in. Shawn dropped me off; he had to go to work. Dave was leaving work early to take me home. I explained my symptoms to the nurse practitioner in the Urgent Care department. She agreed with our neighbor that it was most likely vertigo, but she needed to confirm. She asked me to lie down on the examining table. Holy crap, that was bad. Then she turned my head, which caused such a severe episode, so much so that both my arms reached out for stability. One hit the wall, the other I am sure left a bruise on her arm from my death-grip attempt to stop the spinning.

"I'll need to do that again on the other side" was the next thing I heard her say.

That received an, "Oh hell no!" response from me. "Whatever it is, I have it. We are not doing that again!"

She explained that I had BPPV, which is caused by dislodged crystals in my inner ear. About that time, Dave walked in. He'd had vertigo for several years, so he understood what meds and steps were necessary. I listened, trying to pay attention, but thinking, *'I do not have time for this!'*

Her final words: "This may take three days to three months to resolve itself. Some people have success with physical therapy. Please follow up with your primary care physician if you are not better next week."

It didn't go away in three days, or three months. It only got better when Wendy, my amazing "dizzy doc," worked her magic six months later. She spent most of that first appointment and all of the second appointment explaining how the ears and eyes impact balance, and asking questions about my medical history. Contrary to popular belief, it has nothing to do with fluids in the ears and Meclizine (a common treatment) can just make it worse. She asked if I had migraines, any history of head injuries, neurological issues, sleep disorders, or high stress levels. This was followed by, "was this your first episode of vertigo?"

As we talked, she told stories about the last twenty years of treating people with different types of dizzy and how our beliefs, behaviors, and attitudes affect our health. Stress changes our brain chemistry, which alters our ability to function in many ways.

In addition to her magic procedure, I also learned a few exercises to calibrate my eyes and balance. But the majority of her therapy was dealing with the causes of stress. Unfortunately, there was no way to tell if or when the BPPV will come back, but I know how to put the crystals in my inner ear back where they belong. She continued to emphasize that reducing stress and increasing exercise were the best ways to prevent future episodes.

It's funny how that theme of reducing stress and increasing exercise kept repeating itself in my life. When I thought back on other major health events in my life, extreme stress was the one constant. I had always considered myself healthy and extremely active. I walk faster than most and prefer activities that do not require sitting for long periods of time. When I did get sick, though, it was extreme enough to keep me down for weeks, not days. Wendy became the newest member of my support system, highlighting exactly what I needed to hear, when I needed to hear it.

I can attribute most of my success to lessons learned from a select group of strong women in my personal and professional life. My mom was the first and still is one of the most influential of them. Doing what is right, even when difficult, has changed my life for the better. She taught me that. As a teenager hellbent on getting out of high school early, I had a masterful plan: be an exchange student and spend my senior year in a foreign county. Six weeks into an eleven-month program, I called begging to come home.

That phone call took six hours to get an international line, costing me $110.00. What did my mom say? "Buck up, this was your plan. We do not quit," and she hung up!

Today, when I complain about teenagers, she reminds me how much fun I was at the same age. Decisions have consequences, sometimes good, sometimes bad. You own the consequences and no one else should take the blame or glory. Opportunities are earned with hard work and tenacity. Make the best of an uncomfortable situation by finding something positive provides time to problem-solve and move forward. Being grateful, rather than entitled, is the hardest lesson to explain.

Living in a developing nation, as an American, with an extremely wealthy host family, exceeded all my expectations. Witnessing extreme poverty and extreme excess was a bit mind-blowing for an American teenager in the seventies. The lack of services, safety, security, color television, and peanut butter was contrasted with servants, private school, private planes, vacation homes, and a Jaguar sedan complete with a driver. The militaristic government, cops with machine guns, drug cartels, and the threat of kidnapping helped me decide to keep my head low, learn as much as I could, take lots of pictures, and survive my self-inflicted situation.

Since then, that "never quit; find a new solution" mantra has served me well. When it became clear that studying Architecture at the University of Illinois was not working out, I found a different Architecture program in Texas. By the time I had in-state residency, I figured out that Accounting was more marketable, and changed my major. Over the years, I've learned to be grateful that, no matter how bad it gets in America, it could always be worse. I could be stuck in Colombia.

By the early 1990s, I was married with my first two children. Doctors had told me the stress created health issues, but I was focused mainly on changing a bad environment. Stomach issues seemed a minor price to pay to get through a nasty divorce and custody battle . . . still, not as bad as Colombia. On a mission to provide a better life for my family, I worked very hard to make up for the first failed marriage, connecting my older children, Lexi and Clayton, with the rest of their family and moving up the corporate ladder, to take on more responsibility, (and, with it, more stress).

Accounting led me to banking and data processing, which then opened doors to logistics. A systems operator job at a warehouse in Bloomington, Illinois, progressed over twenty-two years into senior management. I enjoyed the challenges, learning about myself, and helping others become more productive. Plus, my facilities made a positive impact on the community, my home, and work families.

I was also ready to expand my family with my second husband. By 2001, life became more exciting when, finally, the In Vitro Fertilization (IVF) cycles worked. That's how my twins came into this world (self-inflicted multiples).

Pregnancy is physically stressful, twins multiply the risk, and when you add a maternal age of forty-one? BINGO. Complications.

This Wonder Woman did not put up her cape. I kept working as long as possible, even with gestational diabetes and on bedrest. Sitting still, and worse, having someone else take care of my responsibilities, was worse than the sixty-five-pound weight gain. Intent on maintaining throughout the pregnancy, I ignored warning signs and Shawn and Jonathan were born at thirty-five weeks, considered full-term, weighing just five pounds each, but no Neonatal Intensive Care Unit was necessary for them.

I did not bounce back as expected. Instead, complications from Congestive Heart Failure (CHF) landed *me* in the ICU. Thankfully, a great support system (my mom and mother-in-law) plus an amazing hospital staff in Lake Forest, Illinois, made sure all three of us survived. Physical recovery took nearly six months, even though I felt ready after four months. The doctors would not release me to work until they were absolutely sure.

It was my first wakeup call.

My return to work was never in question. I had a great job, the resources to pay for a nanny until the boys were two, and a wonderful daycare facility after that, but something was missing at my work. It didn't feel the as fulfilling as it once had. The thought of changing companies seemed nearly impossible. because there's one thing I've left out of this story: I never finished a bachelor's degree in accounting or any other major. I worked so hard and performed so well that I never needed one. I was consistently achieving better metrics, had happy customers and employees, and gained more margin . . . for less pay than my male counterparts, even those without a degree. For the first time, it felt wrong. It was time to earn that bachelor's degree.

The rise in online education provided a possibility. During a holiday week in Florida, my mom and I researched online programs available in 2004. DePaul University had a program designed specifically for working adults that acknowledged all previous college credits and workplace learning. Their competency-based curriculum maximized past work; nearly all of my credits, decades old, were accepted. The very first class at DePaul introduced adult education theories along with creating a degree plan and selecting a mentor. Selecting a mentor was an eye-opening exercise.

It was wakeup call number two.

The process of mentoring was very specific. The mentor must have a master's degree and be someone you respect and can learn from. I considered myself a mentor to several of my employees, however, I could not think of anyone at that specific time in my company who met the requirements for me. That's when reflective learning, a key component in all DePaul coursework, kicked in. I really stopped to think about the people who had influenced my life and my career, and I knew finishing the degree was even more important. Throughout my career, I would normally do my own research when problem-solving, by reading business, logistics, and leadership books and going to seminars. It never dawned on me to ask for help from senior managers. This lifelong learning described my problem-solving and management style; more importantly, it explained why I did not fit into my company's culture. Always the idealist, I continued to do my best, even in bad circumstances, knowing I did have a ticket out of my existing career when I finished my degree.

Closing one of our facilities turned out to be a role I'd have to fill until that ticket out could be cashed in. It was one of the worst situations. Many factors, internal and external, resulted in a service contract backed by a thirteen-year relationship, being awarded to a competitor. Only our newest employees, making the least money, were offered temporary positions. My work family, more than eighty people, were either out of a job or working without benefits. I spent my last four months before the transition preparing employees with resumes and interview training, documenting processes, and trying to prepare the new vendor for the transition. To everyone's surprise, we closed the facility with as much professionalism and dignity as possible.

I accepted an account management role, with very mixed emotions. I was relieved to have a job, worried about a new travel expectation, jaded by the realization that exceeding expectations is not always enough to keep a facility open, worried for those without jobs, and wondering how to navigate the politics of senior management.

Wakeup call number three occurred three years into my account management role. While hosting a conference call with participants in five time zones and four different countries, my body sent me a message. It wasn't really pain – just a bizarre sensation of numbness, tingling, and pressure. Because of the prior CHF, everyone was concerned. Two days in the hospital and several tests concluded no issues with my heart. The doctors had no explanation; most likely it was a panic attach caused by stress and hormones. Ultimately, I requested and was granted a severance package, as the work environment and travel schedule were making me physically ill.

What a relief!

I spent the summer catching up with friends and family and enrolled in the fall semester to finish my bachelor's degree in Corporate Training and Organizational Development. Finishing the college goal, started so many years ago, was very important to me. Focusing on family and learning was such a pleasant change; it gave my mind and body time to heal and catch up. Each class required research, writing, and reading to demonstrate learning. When possible, I incorporated research on health and nutritional impacts on wellness. Reflective learning was integrated into each course, giving me time to think back on situations, causes, resolutions, and alternatives. Common themes were appearing in my education; lifelong learning, stewardship, service, ethics, and critical thinking. There were also themes of consistently delivering preferable outcomes.

Shortly after graduating, I hoped consulting (i.e., self-employment) was a better path than the corporate world. The idea of returning to a corporate job had lost all appeal. I embraced starting a consulting business with the goal of helping local business owners solve problems and save money. I quickly discovered that I found it very difficult to approach strangers, even when I knew how to help. It became painfully obvious that sales training would be required to run a successful consulting business. At this point, most people expected me to get a corporate job. It would have been easier, but I knew in my heart that the easy way was rarely the best way for me. *'Practice what you preach, walk the walk, lead by example, and do what is in your heart,'* were the messages running through my head every time I felt like throwing in the towel.

Being self-employed afforded me the opportunity to volunteer at church, chair the boys' scout pack, support the boys' scout troop, attend soccer and football games, and volunteer at the boys' middle school. Service was very rewarding and it restored my sense of accomplishment, offsetting the drunk monkey failure self-talk. This was, maybe, the first time I realized the importance of having a great support system.

I'm not sure exactly why, but a *Rich Dad* real estate class shortly after graduation really peaked my interest, introducing the concept of multiple streams of income, and opening up a whole new world of opportunities. My parents had a very lucrative rental property portfolio; most of my corporate roles included contract and facility management; and architecture was my dream job and first college major. Finally, this could be a way to follow my passion, contribute, and build a business with the potential to employ and support my family. Remarkably, several of the people I met at those first real estate classes are now agents at Keller Williams where I work today.

The boys' first year of high school introduced new challenges and real estate investing showed some small progress with one property leased and a few property management projects. These wins, along with a property management project for our church, kept me very busy. The thought of the twins going to college had me considering a master's in educational leadership and a job working for a university to help offset some of the tuition costs.

By Christmas of their freshman year, it became clear I was the one willing to do the most work so they could go to college. Maybe it was too much to expect; maybe I was putting too much pressure on them; the more I pushed, the more they rejected any direction. Homework was skipped and sport practices were missed. After significant frustration (and a bit of counseling), I made a complete about face, changed my major to Organizational Leadership, put the consulting on the back burner, and signed up to get my real estate license.

Looking back, it was kind of a temper tantrum, my way of demonstrating the consequences of choices, both good and bad. As hard as it was, I had to let both of my sons own their own consequences of skipping practice and blowing off homework. I'm not sure who was more shocked – the boys or their teachers. Raising teenagers takes patience and a sense of humor, which I lost more times than I care to admit. Watching extremely intelligent boys waste talents and time created an internal battle. Emotionally, I wanted to help them; logically, I knew they had to develop their own motivations. The internal and external battles continued. Some days I won; other days I lost my temper, but not my mind.

Shortly after passing my real estate exam, I got a message from a business partner telling me he had joined Keller Williams (KW) as an agent; he and I had attended that first *Rich Dad* class, together. When he learned that I, too, had passed the exam, he asked which KW office I was with. In reality, I hadn't done my research and had just picked a company where a friend worked.

"Your degree is in training, how could you go anywhere else," my friend asked, knowing that KW valued training and education as I had for all my years. It only took a few meetings with the office's team leader and waiting for my first transaction to close, before I switched to Keller Williams in the fall of 2017.

The culture, training, and atmosphere is based on the same values and principals I believe are necessary for a successful business. Having the tools and models to build a real estate business based on sound research enables growth no mater your focus. Reflecting on my first year at KW, I set my annual goal without considering the amount of time needed to finish my master's course work, nor did I consider the learning curve associated with new systems and processes. I especially did not anticipate the vertigo episode just as the market and my business were taking off. The reality was I'd been "out of balance" for a lot longer than the day it smacked me down on my knees in my living room.

◆　◆　◆

June was wakeup call number four.

Yes, I'm a slow learner. It was time to put up my wonder woman cape and stop trying to do it all. First, I had to tell the folks at church that I could not organize the annual auction I had run in the past; then I delegated most of my scouting responsibilities; and finally Dave and the boys took over I most of household duties. It was all I could do to keep up with the real estate transactions on my plate, so additional schooling also had to take a back seat.

Luckily, Dave's mom spent six weeks in July and August herding my teenagers. By the time school started, I was feeling somewhat better, but not yet back to normal. Most of the summer transactions were closing up and I did not have the bandwidth to add more customers. I made a conscious decision to find some balance . . . both mental and physical.

I wonder why the thought of going to physical therapy in June was so distressing. After talking to Wendy, even though she could have made the vertigo go away shortly after the first episode, I really needed this wake-up call . . . all of the wakeup calls . . . to truly understand the impact stress was having on my body.

The strong support system from my corporate life, while not officially mentors, made a lasting impact. I was taught tenacity, laughter, and professional skills as much as I was taught golf, good wine, and negotiating. These pseudo-mentors, mostly women, brought me enthusiasm, energy, and project management. Women from school, work, and church have taught me about community, faith, and running my business. (In full disclosure, I have a village of men, including my own family, who are strong and hard-working, too.)

With education, hard-work, acceptance of mentors, sharing the load of day-to-day life, my health, and a cape-less approach to business, I am well on my way to finding balance. For me, this is best described as: **Live, Love, Learn, Laugh and Leave a Legacy**.[1]

---

[1] * Covey, Stephen R. 1999. Living the 7 Habits: Stories of Courage and Inspiration, Page 292, Simon & Schuster, New York, NY.

"The best view comes after

the toughest climb."

~ Unknown

LIFE

◆ ◆ ◆

Life has worth when you are content, happy, living your best life, and you feel rewarded and fulfilled. Maybe this is when family relationships are strong and healthy. Maybe it's when you are living a balanced work and home life. Is it when you are confident and feeling your best because you are making health, fitness, and spiritual life a top priority?

For many, the most fulfilling time is when they are in pursuit of goals. They thrive on challenges and feel worthiest when finding solutions and growing stronger from experiences and opportunities. There is pride in conquering and achieving a goal one sets for himself or herself. Life – life worth living – is most rewarding when full of gratitude and being valued by others. Inspiring and mentoring others in reaching their goals also adds to your own life feeling like one worth living!

◆ ◆ ◆

"Be. Do. Have."

~ kw MAPS BOLD LAWS

Scott Klaas is the Operating Principal of KW Milwaukee SW and also co-leads a Real Estate Sales Team. He is honored to be a part of this project because he wanted to dig deeper into what drives him so he can be a better leader to others. He is committed to bring out The Big Why in others to help them reach their full potential despite of their fears. He lives in New Berlin, WI with his wife Nicole of 10 years and 2 kids Samantha (5) and Benjamin (3) where they enjoy down time, play dates & cheering on the Bucks, Brewers, Badgers & Packers.

CLARITY AND CONNECTION

Scott Klaas

◆ ◆ ◆

T*ICK-TICK-TICK.*
My ten-minute drive home usually consists of these thoughts:
'If I just work hard enough, then I can have some thinking time.'
'If I can get caught up, then I will feel amazing.'
'This is the way it is and, one day, I will see the fruits of my labor.'
'I just need tonight to work through this, and then I will be an amazing father and husband (when it is done).'
'Once the kids are asleep, I will drink a monster energy drink and stay up as long as I can.'

My daily task list gets longer and longer and, after my drive home, reality sets in. I get home and lug in my backpack filled with everything I am going to magically get done today and I put it on the counter. I search for the kids and smile and laugh and pretend I'm a monster and tell them how much I love them. I get changed and mindlessly snack on whatever is in front of me until dinner is done. I wonder how I'm going to have the energy to make it to the kids' bedtime. I yell at Ben for taking Sam's toy. I get unnecessarily testy for a simple question asked by my wife, Nicole. I scream out loud for Sammy to pick up her room.

I need to sit down. My phone numbs my mind like a drug. I check Facebook, text messages, emails . . . anything that makes sense – anything that will give me that shot of dopamine or adrenaline that will lift me up to do what I have to do. I tell myself to put my phone away and I start to make a smoothie. My kids love to push the buttons that make the blender go. I fill the container up with everything, seal it and shake it so the ice rattles. The kids come running like some weird science experiment. I laugh every time. Each one wants to get to the blender first so they can push the first three buttons (second place pushes the last three). They would stop a personal visit from Micky or Minnie Mouse to win this race. This feels amazing. The energy doesn't last long. I go and sit on the couch. Ben brings me my phone as he sees me on it a lot and wants to be helpful. I yell at him, "No Benny, I don't want to have my phone now. I am going to play with you." *'Well, since it's here . . .'* I check for anything new since I put it down five minutes ago . . . the addiction continues.

This is an unwinnable battle
There is no finish line.
It is like spinning around on a hamster wheel.

I work harder than most everyone I know and yet I get nowhere. I can barely keep my eyes open and the thought of playing or being my goofy self seems overwhelming. I look at the clock and it is only 7:14 P.M. I need to make it until 8:15 and then I can put them to bed and start my second workday.

I lay down on the ground and tell the kids to play jail. They come running over like it is the most fun game on Earth as they bury me by piling pillows on my head and I lay there yelling "Nooooo!" and "Helllllllp!"

They laugh like I'm the best dad in the world, but all I feel is guilt that I figured out a way to scam the system. They think it's great while I am just really too lazy to do anything else other than doze in and out of consciousness. I wake up and they are both gone. Sammy is watching the iPad and Ben is playing with his Paw Patrol tower on his own. I look at the clock and it is 8:30. Bedtime!

It is my turn to put Sammy to bed, however Ben is always faster for me to put to sleep and extremely hard for Nicole. I yell from the living room floor my bed time negotiations. If I put Ben to sleep, will you brush his teeth and get his jammies on? Nicole jumps at the opportunity and I plop down on the rocking chair. He grabs six books from his book shelf and hands them to me. I read the shortest one and he asks for more books. I read another one and instantly turn off the light. He asks for more books. I tell him tomorrow I will read more and that it's time for bed. When I have more energy, I will read him more. We both fall asleep on the rocking chair.

At 9:45 P.M., I wake up, put him on his bed and somehow manage my way across my house to my bedroom. This is always the hardest part of the day. It may as well be four football fields long as it takes every bit of energy to get there. I walk past my bag and the mound of work I was going to get done and tell myself I will wake up early instead of staying up late. I plop down on my bed. I need two minutes and then I will brush my teeth.

Tomorrow will be different.

How is it even possible that I am here right now and how did it happen so fast?

The days turn into weeks, the weeks into months, the months into years, and the years into decades. The irony is that I spend my life trying not to waste time *thinking*, but in these couple of days, this is all I have been able to do.

I am perfectly comfortable with the morphine drip and I feel nice and warm under the blankets. I can say I am pain-free, however I have come to the conclusion that my time here is very limited and I am being haunted by the ticking of the seconds on the clock on the wall. Like most of us, I have been in a battle with time and hearing the *TICK-TICK-TICK* is a constant reminder that I have not lived my story the way I would have chosen to write it.

Scrooge and *Click*: two of my favorite movies pop into my head. They both have the same theme of getting a second chance to live their lives differently at the end. I close my eyes as I realize I will not be getting that second chance. I think of how much my friends and I laughed when we saw that sign on the wall of the bar that read, "Free Drinks Tomorrow." *'Tomorrow.'*

It's a hard pill to swallow when you realize you've had over 20,000 tomorrows to get it right and you never truly figured it out. We all have 50,000 to 70,000[2] thoughts in our head every day and up to ninety-eight percent of them are the same thoughts we had the day before[3], but which have not been changed, pursued, or dealt with.

Then comes a brand-new thought: *'What is it about my life that is going to outlive me?'*

---

[2] *https://www.huffpost.com/entry/healthy-relationships_b_3307916*

[3] *http://www.jenniferhawthorne.com/articles/change_your_thoughts.html*

The answers both fill me with joy and make me sad. Those who love me will say their goodbyes and the last thought I'll have is that I am not done writing my story. The weight of this seems so real . . . that it instantly jolts me awake.

As I rub my eyes and stretch, I get recombobulated to where I am. I see my wife and dog sleeping peacefully. I realize I do get a second chance! I am thirty-six years old and have an extremely busy day ahead of me. Starting tomorrow I will really get this nailed down. Then I laugh to myself and pull out my calendar to see what I can reschedule to give me what I suddenly want most in the world . . . time to think!

For more than two decades, I haven't taken the time out to adequately listen to what my subconscious was telling me and now I feel a brand-new type of pain. It isn't the nagging sports injuries, the feeling of tightness, or the everyday aches of being 6'8". This is different; it is like my soul hurts. It is impossible to describe other than by saying that there is something inside of me that wants to be heard and that voice is becoming more and more demanding that I take the time to listen. This journey is going to start today and it both frightens me and excites me to see what I am going to learn when I open Pandora's box. It's time to start a sixty-six-day challenge to build a habit out of thinking time.

It doesn't take me long to realize that the past two and a half years have taught me that I am mortal. I lost my mother to cancer and my older brother committed suicide. My default mode has been to plow through without giving this much thought because it's easier that way. There are random moments when a memory will come back or a picture will be seen and I shed some tears.

Those moments are few and far between.

The most common thought is how strange it feels to go from a family of five to a family of three in such a short amount of time. I see photos on my wall and it brings back the great memories we had. The funny thing about photos is you only remember the good parts. When looking back, humans have a very unique ability to remember the good and forget the bad. We are all mostly good and doing the best that we know how to do. If we get past the judgement and the gossip, we can really see another person's good, too, and I believe that will outlive us.

◆ ◆ ◆

My mother needed help to understand what she could do in retirement. My dad was retired and enjoying it, however she felt that she would be bored. *'How in the world could anyone think this way,'* I thought?

Bored is a word that I just know nothing about. I could fill forty-eight-hour days as easy as twenty-four. I urged mom to take the leap into retirement. Not long after she made the decision, I received the dreaded phone call.

"Are you sitting down?"

"Yes." (This can't be good. Technically I was sitting down; I just didn't tell them that I was driving home.)

The only words I heard were, "I have cancer."

At the time, I always thought of cancer as something that happened to other people. It was like watching a natural disaster rip through a city on TV. It is always real, it just isn't real for me. This was my first encounter with cancer of someone who was close to me. It was the start of a four-year-plus battle that brought out a strength that was unlike anything I have ever seen. The first response for people to have is to go into victim-mode: *'Why me?'* they will ask.

My mom often said, "Why not me?"

In the hardest of the years, I never heard her speak a complaint. It taught me that you cannot always choose the circumstance, however you can always choose your response. After mom's eight-hour hysterectomy, she was hardly able move and it hurt her to swallow as she was chewing her ice chips. She had the whole family all laughing as she was cracking jokes and imitating someone we knew who gave the worst hugs. She said, "Sorry I'm going to have to give a Jerry hug."

Mom always made it easier for everyone *else*. Her strength gave so many others strength. We put together a book titled *Your Impact on the World* and it was a compilation of stories about her from those who loved her the most. It is so amazing what we remember about people when they are gone. One was deeply affected by the simple moment twenty-five years ago of my mom fixing the buttons on her shirt before school. Many told stories of how our home made them feel safe when growing up:

"I vividly remember being picked up from second grade on a sunny day and playing Ninja Turtles on the Nintendo® in my freshly cleaned and vacuumed room. Then, I was brought in cool ranch Doritos™ and root beer and asked how my day was. There was something so perfectly right about this moment . . . something that made me feel loved and important."

'What if we made it our goal to fill our whole life creating these moments?'

Mom's last real conversation to me was that she was going to regret not being able to see my kids grow up. To me, that is not regret, but a reflection of the relationship mom had already built. She lived every moment they were alive showing them that there was no one else more important to her and she made a lifelong impact on my then-three-year old.

My brother, Robert, was truly one of a kind. I idolized him growing up like any younger brother does. It would be so cool when I could hang out with him or he would spend the night back at home when he was in college. I remember playing cards with him and his friends. I must have been thirteen when they were nineteen. We were playing at our parents' kitchen table and I was on a hot streak. I don't recall the amount of money I was up, yet it felt like all of King Midas's gold . . . and his friends were not too happy with me. Right after the biggest win of the night, my dad came in and told me it was time for bed. Bob's head tilted back and he let out a bellowing laugh as his friends swore and yelled that this was BS. How did a thirteen-year-old take all of their money and then have a perfectly planned exit before they had a chance to win it back? Two things stick out most to me about that night: 1) his friends have still never let the loss go and, 2) my brother had the world's greatest laugh. His laugh was the kind that must have burned 1,000 calories every time just from the pure physical spectacle it was.

Robert, or Bob to me, was an overall shy person who could transform into someone without a care in the world. He could really open up around those he felt comfortable with. We would go to movies, trade basketball cards, and pick on our sister. Although I always knew Bob was shy, it still shocked me when my dad told me that he went in to see a therapist. I paused, not knowing what to say. I told him, "No way." That is the same day that I saw a therapist, as well.

For two sons who had a father battling bipolar disorder, we sure weren't very eager to admit that we were both going through some tough times, too. We just handled it differently. He went internal and I became louder and more of a comedian. If I'm laughing and making other people laugh, then I am not thinking about how I feel. Coming to terms with my coping mechanisms was a long and draining process. It allowed me to understand who I am and get a better handle on my life. My case was milder; I managed without being on medication for very long. While I was getting better, though, my brother was getting worse. His extreme manic episodes partnered with schizophrenia ended his marriage, ended his career, got him in trouble with the law, and ultimately took away nearly a decade of his life.

Nowhere in *this* Bob was a hint of the Bob of old.

He was unrecognizable and left to mostly a life of solitude – a place where he could let his mind run free to create a false reality in his head. This fake truth was manifested and fueled over time because what you focus on expands. Somehow, he managed to find the strength to work out of his inner hell.

Bob started to work out consistently; he was taking care of himself again; and he became a loving uncle to his niece Samantha and later, his nephew, Ben. He got his personality back, he started working again, and he was building a great relationship as tricky Uncle Ba Ba. We even got to see "the laugh" multiple times. Things were turning around for the better and it was unbelievable.

He would have his days, like anyone else, yet he was on the right path. That is, until the day I got a missed call from my sister in the afternoon. Then I got a call from my dad. *'Ok, something definitely isn't right.'*

Dad told me that Bob had committed suicide. It didn't make sense. *'How could that be? Five years ago, there would have been no surprise, but now?'*

Telling Samantha turned out to be harder that I thought. She knew all too well what heaven meant. Cleaning out his apartment, the only pictures we found were on his fridge; they were my Christmas Card and photos of my kids. This made me stop in my tracks. My kids meant the world to him. What stands out to me now isn't that he would be the first in line to eat all the cheesy potatoes at family functions or that he put his wet shoes up on our couch. It is how remarkably strong and caring he was to fight the battle he fought. Reading his journals gave me insights into how his mind worked and it helped me to understand what an amazing spirit he had.

Voices would tell him to do things and he was smart and caring enough to not listen. In the end, it was (in his mind) a true act of sacrifice for the greater good of humanity and not depression that got to him. All the time he spent during the last decade gave his mind plenty of time to create a false reality. It turned out to be too much and he had the strength to carry out an act that he truly believed would save us all. At his funeral, his pastor said he lived his life like Jesus; it turned out he ended it like Jesus, as well.

Mental Health is such a taboo topic.

Nearly everyone on this planet struggles with anxiety, depression, doubt, anger, and more at some point in their lives. Some are just biologically predisposed to having it affect them more. There should be no shame to it. If there were more of an openness to the subject, then it would not be allowed to have the level of effect that it does. There is no simple answer to solving the issue, yet having clarity of purpose and confidence in your self-worth at an early age would help control it before it could fully take root and create lies in your heart and mind. I am passionate about bringing this out in people. I am not naive enough to think it is a cure-all; however, I feel that knowing purpose and self-worth could help this plague dramatically.

'I need to start a charity around this. Maybe I could call it the clarity charity . . . shoot I googled that and it's already taken.'

My mission in life can be to live in this purpose-clarifying way and to show other people that it can be done. Nothing frustrates me more than seeing one of my real estate agents know they should be at Keller Williams, but not act because of fear – fear of change, fear of failure, fear of getting out of their comfort zones. I have seen the changes in people who come over and plug in to what we are teaching. They always say the same thing: "Man I wish I would have done this a year ago when we first talked. Thanks for not giving up on me. I am on the right path to hitting my full potential." It's like I found the light in them that they couldn't find on their own.

Wow!

There is nothing that charges me up more!

But why?

It's a musty smelling and dimly lit visitor's locker room. Everything feels cold and unwelcoming. We are getting dressed for the biggest basketball game of my career as it is the Sectional Final game against our cross-town rival, Madison West. Whoever wins this game is going to state. DMX is blaring in the background as we always bring our own sound system to get pumped up.

"Y'ALL GONNA MAKE ME LOSE MY MIND, UP IN HERE, UP IN HERE."

I am pumping myself up with self-talk. Today is going to be different; today is the day. I'm the senior captain and taller than anyone on the court. It is finally my time to shine. Playing at state, we will be on TV and no one will ever be able take that away from me. We huddle up as a team before taking the court. I have 1,000 things I want to say to pump up my team and myself. Nothing comes out and Glenn Olsen does the talking. I think to myself, '*what am I so afraid of?*' and I call myself a wuss.

We rush out there mentally hopped up and ready for victory. Our modus operandi is to go out to the center of the court to huddle and mosh as a team before tip-off. We soon find out that West has the same plan and both teams are at center court jumping up and down screaming, chanting as if we are all on the same team. It was a euphoric high that can only come from sports and when the biggest gym in the area is jam packed with standing room only. The problem is, the high went away rapidly as I came back to reality and realized I was no longer a starter for my team.

Through the end of the season and the playoff run, the coaches finally picked up on the fact that I was a different player in the games than I was in practice. They couldn't put their finger on it, yet—as the importance of the games grew—so did the megaphone to my internal dialogue that was focused on my bad performance. Up until now, I didn't mind my role decreasing and my starting spot evaporating. It was a lot less nerve-racking on the bench and I could be one hell of a good teammate. I was the first one to encourage someone else after a mistake and the first one to lay it on myself when I did something bad. I manifested the worst possible player that I could become by constantly thinking of the negative scenarios happening and yelling at myself.

Sitting on the bench made me feel like a coach. My role was smaller, so the outcome of the game wasn't dependent upon me. I would still play and the lesser time made it easier for me to focus and do my best – play my role. As the opening tip was thrown, that was all in the past. I snapped out of it. '*This could be the last high school game I ever play and I need to be out there. How did it come to this?*'

I play sparingly throughout the game and we are always close, yet it feels like we are constantly playing catch-up. It is an eternity of feeling we can win and not ever really believing it is going to happen. The final buzzer sounds and we are on the short end. The players for West go wild; the crowd goes wild; I am here sitting in shock. The reality never sinks in until it is too late. It almost feels paralyzing.

High School Basketball is over.

We are each called up to receive a runner-up medal. I summon the strength to walk up there and accept it. On my way back, I throw it down towards the bleachers. *'Just let me go into the locker room. Better yet, just let me crawl into a hole. Even better yet, let me hop in a time machine and go back three weeks. Things will be different then.'*

We go back into the dingy locker room and nothing feels more welcoming. We are able to be alone – away from the celebration. For High School Boys, it is the one time that it is okay to show emotion and we all break down and cry. I sit with my head in my hands and slowly take each one of my brand-new Air Jordans off and throw them in the garbage can. The feeling of regret in this moment is burned into my soul and rarely will a day go by in my life when I do not think about it, dream about it, or get motivated by never wanting to feel this way again. It is not the losing I regret; it is how we lost. It is knowing that fear got the best of me and—because of that—I let myself and my team down.

◆　◆　◆

I realize I never reached my potential in sports, in teaching, or in real estate sales and that it has been a theme of my life. I am driven now to reach my potential as a leader of our team and our office.

I am striving for deeper connections with people. I have managed to know a lot of people and somehow have very few meaningful relationships that I haven't let fizzle out over time. I want to be known for more than just being a goofball who is loud. I want people to know my heart. Because I am so big physically, I feel I need to be guarded emotionally. I just want to hug everyone, but instead they get a Joe Kool head nod and a "Hey!" I cannot stand small talk. It is meaningless and a constant reminder that we don't really have time for one another.

There has to be a better way.

I would rather there just be a simple, "Hi," than an insincere, "How are you?" to follow. I want to start something in my office that I have been too chicken to ever do. I want to be known for responding with, "tell me something good." Then, every time someone sees me for the first time that day, they know they will have to tell me something good. It could become part of our culture to get us thinking positively. I have never tried it. What if we shared our goal for the day . . . something we need an answer or encouragement for? What if we said *anything* other than "I'm good," followed by the still insincere, "and you?"

I wrestle between my thoughts and my actions every day and imagine what it would feel like to be connecting with people at a deeper level. Think about the culture and the energy that would be created.

It would be contagious!

It would be unique!

It would be amazing!

What I need now is to get the fog lifted from my brain. I need to make it a priority to get myself figured out.

Clarity is almost as high as air on my list of needs right now.

Clarity is power.

Clarity will give me consistency . . . and consistency compounds.

I wish I could pretend that I had the complete answer right now. It is a journey to mastery that I am committed to diving into. What I do know is that I need to begin with the end in mind. I am okay with asking myself the hard questions. *'What would life look like if I did put what is most important first? Could I be known as the guy who knows priorities so well that the knowledge pours out of me everywhere I go?'*

I know that I need to narrow my focus. I am attempting at being everything to everyone. I want to read every book, listen to every podcast, sell every house, attract every agent, teach every class. I have an insatiable thirst for knowledge and influence.

Through this three and a half-year journey that Keller Williams has opened my eyes to, I have completely transformed my mindset and am on a path for massive success. There is so much opportunity at my fingertips. There are great people to meet and masterminding to be done. Facebook can be a never-ending hill to climb to see what everyone is up to. It is exhilarating and exhausting, which will ultimately put me in the hospital or completely burn me out if I continue at this pace.

I have become okay with knowing my limitations. I am more valuable to everyone if I take care of myself and don't try to cheat by working extremely long hours. I can have a massive positive effect on my family, my real estate team and my office if they can get more quality out of me. Right now, everyone is getting about 10% of me.

I need to make a dent in my community before I can make a dent in the world. Attempting to boil the ocean is much harder than boiling a pot of water. It is time I focus on the pot of water. It is time I focus on my *One Thing* that will make everything else easier or unnecessary.

My One Thing is to gain crystal clear clarity around my *Big Why* and base every decision around it.

I need to be comfortable with saying, "no," gracefully. This will allow me to do what I am truly passionate about and empower a legacy to help others to reach their ultimate potentials despite their ultimate fears. I will be their role model to show them how to understand what they truly want and how to have the courage to focus on it . . . until they get it. I want to get people to stop playing the broken tapes in their head and shatter through their limiting beliefs. I want to get to the core of the issue that is stopping them from achieving their purposes, rewire their thinking, and show them that anything is possible.

My influence on others will remain capped only by how much I grow myself. I will think differently so I can show other people how to think differently. I am okay with being patient and systematically living the plan. The thought . . . THINKING – the very thing I had avoided for so long . . . sends a new wave of excitement that I haven't felt in years. I feel like I've taken off a fifty-pound backpack, not the backpack of things to do, but the backpack of things I was too afraid to think and feel.

My breath deepens.

My shoulders relax.

My hands unclench.

Having confidence in my plan has finally given me my Mojo back.

◆　◆　◆

My biggest goal now is to get this whole clarity thing figured out, in order for my father to see it in me. Dad has already given me the greatest lesson of all in how to truly play with my kids. Watching him dedicate every ounce of energy to them every Thursday when he has time with them is inspiring. He lets them lead the fun and plays right along with them. I have been too concerned with making *every* moment the *best* moment, that I do not enjoy the simplicity of having them be children *for the* moment. It is easy for me to take them somewhere big and pump them up; it is hard for me to not have a plan and just play. We have a free babysitter in my dad who travels an hour each way once a week and buys us dinner. It doesn't get much better than that! I laugh every time as he attempts to leave around 6:15 P.M. and gets talked into staying until after 8:00. He has to get ready to leave four or more times and always ends up playing hide and seek or some other game . . . "just *one* more time."

Spending just one day in a carefree manner like this is what I dream about the most. *'What would this truly feel like? Can I give up my responsibilities for one day and truly enjoy the moment?'* I make a decision that this paradise, the paradise of living each moment, is going to happen for me this weekend!

Scott on a carefree family day.

When dad leaves, I think of all the things I want to say: *Thank you, Dad, for giving me such a great foundation and model for what it means to be a true man. I often wonder if you are superhuman. You are so strong. Losing a mom and a brother is tough, yet it has to fail in comparison to losing a wife of forty-seven years and a son. You cheered for me, even when I sat on the bench. You struggled with your own bipolar disorder and somehow overcame the demons*

77

who were whispering lies about your worth. You ask 'how am I?' and mean it, actually waiting for a sincere response. You are inspiration and I don't tell you enough how proud I am of you, how much I love you, and how grateful I am to be your son.'

Instead, I say, "Thank you. drive safe," and "goodbye.'"

It's the morphine drip response while the clock *TICK-TICK-TICKS.*

But it's time to wake up!

This moment has been approaching for a while and I have planned it out and fully accepted it. I am at peace with myself and the way I have lived my life in the past, but it's changing going forward. I am surrounded by those that love me most and have great support from all the people I have helped through the years, from the end of sports, to the losses of mom and Bob.

I think once more about what in my life is going to outlive me. I smile at the thoughts that flow in – the highs like Bob's laugh and mom's "Jerry hug," that live on in memory and the way those memories affect me; the lows, heavy and imprisoning like the pillows piled on by Sam and Ben; and all the lessons along the way from Dad, Nicole, and my team.

I think about the legacy of people who will continue to write *my* story. There is comfort knowing that only the good will be remembered when people look at the pictures in their hallways after I have given my last lesson and taught my last class. My family will have the strength to go on and continue what we have built—a fearless life of clarity and connection.

I close my eyes and drift away to the next chapter . . .

TICK-TICK-TICK.

"Self-confidence is the best

outfit, rock it and own it!"

~ Unknown

Kim Rogne is a twenty-year plus entrepreneur and business leader in real estate. She is the Team Leader of the #1 largest KW real estate office in suburban Milwaukee, Wisconsin. She's passionate about coaching, training, and leading her agents and team to find purposes in why they do what they do so they can take their businesses and personal lives to the next level. With her husband and daughters, she enjoys traveling, skiing, hiking, snorkeling, and anything to embrace her love of nature. She hopes these stories allow readers to realize nobody's life is perfect; however, we grow from personal experiences . . . and have the ability to choose our own lives "worth" living. For more information, visit **www.kwmilwaukeesouthwest.com**.

How A Hairy Situation Shaped My Life

Kim Rogne

"**G**irl, you are so lucky! Your energy is infectious and you are so smart and engaging. I cannot wait to soak you all up and learn from you. And man that *hair* of yours . . . it's insane. Your husband isn't too bad, either. He is so helpful, kind, and caring. How do I grow up to be just like you? Seriously, you are running a real estate company with over 130 agents and you command a room like nobody's business. I wish I had half the smarts and belief in myself as you do. And, did I mention that *hair*! How *do* I get all of that?"

My hair, which is quite often referred to as if it were a separate being, has nothing to do with talent or smarts. Lucky for me, I was born with it. (Though my husband and children would say it's as much a curse as it is a blessing. It clogs the drains and vacuums and basically has a mind of its own. It also, quite literally, adds almost an hour to the morning prep time if I need to wash it.)

My attitude, energy, and career success are *not* things, though, that I was born with, nor were they something that came easily to me. All the success I have in life today is because of a *choice* that I made almost twenty-five years ago and the *choices* I continue to make every day.

Embarrassment.

Shame.

Low self-esteem.

Never feeling smart enough.

Never feeling pretty enough.

Never feeling skinny enough.

I was a person who was never enough of *anything* to *anyone.*

To anyone looking in from the outside, I was known as the pretty and popular one, while—on the inside—I felt like nothing of the sort.

"Congratulations 1991 high school graduates! Your high school years will be your greatest memories and you will never forget how these experiences helped to shape you into who you are today and who you will become in the future."

'High school? Never again,' I say to myself. If I could go back I would change everything about my high school experience . . . *or would I?*

During my high school years, we would go everywhere together in his enormous, four-doored, black, oversized Cadillac® (or something that I thought might have been a Cadillac). I have never been one to know the names of cars and, to this day, if my husband asks what kind of car someone is driving (because apparently knowing whether it is a Ford or a BMW can be immediately recognized by some), I will only be able to tell him the color and if it looks like an SUV, truck, or sedan. I have no idea how to identify it further. His car, though, the one I spent my high school days in, was more than just the color black, it was blackness, itself . . . like entering the pit of a deep, dark, cold, empty hole. He would come pick me up wearing nothing but wrinkled jean shorts and an on-trend, 1990s, armpit cut-out tank top with all of his (overly mature), teenage, "manly," black hair poking out everywhere. No shoes; he would never wear shoes. He would drive around all day with no shoes on! It was so gross!

The car smelled like a high school boys' locker room: wreaking of bologna sandwiches and bad body odor. He would slow down just enough for me to open the big, creaky passenger door, so that I could slide over the leather seat and scoot up next to his side. Thinking about this today makes me want to puke! Me by his side like he was my prince and I his princess joining him in his carriage. Nothing could be further from the truth. What control and abuse can make you believe is scary . . . and what others didn't see happening behind those closed car doors was an even scarier secret.

"If you get out of this car, I will run you over!" he warned.

As a young, naïve, sixteen-year-old girl, his words rang in my head like a lightning bolt. I froze, not daring to move, and remained like a statue in the front seat of his car. I felt like a scolded child.

"You are nothing without me and you know it!"

He was smart; I am talking Ivy League college smart. With his thick, jet-black hair, sought after manly mustache that every teenage boy wished they could grow, and his broad shoulders that took hours of weightlifting to accomplish, he was able to fool some into believing he was in at least his early twenties. I had football games to watch him play in and parties to attend every weekend with friends. What more would a teenage girl want?

"Don't you ever leave me, because—if you do—I will hurt you. You are nothing without me and you know it."

Being the oldest of three girls, my sisters and I were frequently referred to as the "pretty one," the "smart one," and the "athletic one." We were boxed into these characters we were supposed to play. Yes, you guessed it; I was obligated to fill the role of the pretty one. I was already born with the hair, so I might as well play it up. Why I couldn't be the smart one *and* the pretty one, I will never know. In my messed up teenage head, I could only be one character and I would fulfill that role to a T.

Left to right, the athlete, the beauty, the brains.

I had big Aquanet® hair sprayed curls, wore brand name, mall-bought clothes (and wouldn't dare wear anything from Sears or K-Mart), owned a Swatch® watch and hung around with the wealthiest kids in town. This well-formed display was what made me who I was. This perfect façade was also an easy way to mask the truth.

I grew up in a small, traditional, Wisconsin town with hard-working parents who provided me with a secure, loving home. I know my parents couldn't have realized the truth of what my high school boyfriend relationship was all about or they would have stepped in. I do, however, remember an incident when one of my younger sisters threatened to throw her pet rock at him if he didn't stop yelling at me. That was the extent of the abuse "showing up" and revealing itself to my family.

When you're in an abusive situation, your self-worth is so low, that you don't even know you can go to somebody for help, support, and escape. I didn't tell anyone because I felt as much at fault as my abuser. No. more. This isn't a story of blame, nor a story of wanting redemption from the high school boy who abused me. It's about who I was: a girl who was secretly both physically and emotionally abused, but who chose not to let that season define her.

I thought I would grow up to be nothing but a useless stupid object that would only be good for one thing: show up pretty, well-behaved, and voiceless on the arm of my prince. Instead, I took the awful *reality* of my relationship experience and used it to truly become a better person. I hope someone reading this who lived through such an experience will choose to forgive and purposefully write her own story, rather than having someone else write it for her.

I don't exactly remember when the control and abuse started. Funny how that happens. I remember when it was bad, but how it got there? I can't remember the exact moment in time when I became his puppet and lost my self-worth. *'When did he first say something hurtful? When did he hit me?'* I can't remember the specific date I thought I needed *him* in order to be a whole person. I hadn't grown up with abuse, but—for some reason—because I wasn't abused daily, I thought it was acceptable. I do remember trying to leave this lie of a picture-perfect relationship multiple times. I remember him crying, honestly . . . I mean tears and all; he told me he needed me and I needed him, and that he would never hurt me again. He told me that he would take care of me for the rest of my life.

I believed him.

It was another lie – another secret.

The ultimate shame and embarrassment comes when someone sees that dirty little secret. It happened for me one day in that black hole of a car.

"How many times do I have to tell you, don't ever change the station?!"
SLAP!

There we were again in his big, black, four-door shithole. It was after a school activity, sitting in the back seat, was one of my dearest friends from elementary school that I hadn't spoken to in years. She and I used to spend every waking moment together. We built forts and had sleepovers where we secretly watched R-rated movies like *Friday the 13th*; we ate Cheetos® and Oreos® all night and, when back at school the next week, we would write notes in a shared notebook decorated with stickers and dreams of who we would date someday. Then, we turned thirteen and entered middle school. I was part of the popular gang, she wasn't, and—just like that—our friendship was no more.

Now in high school and feeling a bit more mature, I was excited to reconnect with her and was hoping we could rekindle our lost friendship. As my boyfriend drove her home from school, a simple radio station change resulted in the angry slap in front of someone else.

I wonder what she was thinking while witnessing me and my abuser from the back seat. Maybe she thought that I was too stupid for either not listening to him or for allowing him to do that to me. Out of shame and embarrassment, I made the decision right then and there that I would never talk to her again. Isolation with my secret. I chose it. It wasn't imposed. I prayed that no one would find out. There would be no rekindling of that friendship and I chose to barely make eye contact with her ever again.

The incident wasn't the only time I was shamed in public.

"Pick up your books yourself!"

KICK!

My books were slapped out of my hands and kicked across the school hallway. Did I say the wrong thing? Did I wear the wrong thing? Did I talk to someone he didn't approve of? Who knows what the reasoning was behind this burst of abuse, but there it was happening in public for others to see between classes at school. I quickly swept my books up into my arms, looked around, and prayed that no one would see. Everyone would surely laugh at me and think I was such a loser. Never once did I think someone would see and want, or even need, to help.

The Homecoming Queen and her hair.

Somehow, I became the master magician and kept the abuse to myself. He was the star football player; I the popular cheerleader; we were the cutest dating couple who eventually became the Homecoming King and Queen. It almost sounds made up, but sadly this was my nonfiction life in my high school years. I had to keep this image going and alive no matter what the consequences to my physical and emotional being were.

Between the ages of fifteen and eighteen and a half, I was repeatedly spit on, slapped (though never leaving a bruise in a place for anyone else to see), told I was stupid, and punished if I hung out with the so-called wrong people. I reluctantly lost my virginity in the back seat of that haunting, big, black, disgusting boat of a car (*man I hated that car!*) and who knows whatever else happened given that I have buried so much deep down in my memory bank.

The truth is that the words hurt me more than any of the physical abuse ever did. A bruise can heal, but years of degrading words and putdowns burn on the brain until they take over your internal self-worth. His words literally showed up on the outside and became part of every fiber in my body. I deeply believed I *had to* marry this boy because I was never going to amount to anything without him. He was going to get his Ivy League college education which would guarantee a high-paying career and, because I wasn't smart enough to amount to anything, I didn't need to complete college, anyway. I could be his adoring beautiful wife and have his babies. He would provide me with everything I needed to live the picture-perfect dream.

That was the plan, anyway.

In 1991, after high school graduation, I went to a Wisconsin State University and he flew off to attend the Ivy League school he'd always planned on. We would continue dating long distance, which worked on and off for about the next year and a half. Back then, there were no cell phones with facetime or other forms of social media, so maintaining a long-distance relationship was quite challenging.

It was a blessing in disguise.

During my freshman year in College nobody knew what was happening to me on the inside. There was this lingering aftermath of the hateful words continuing to ring in my head: *'You aren't smart enough and you will never amount to anything!'*

I felt like a fraud. *'What was I doing in college? I am not smart enough to be here.'* Don't get me wrong, I embraced the social freedom of college with no problem: partying, smoking, drinking, making new friends, and getting a chance to fool around with boys was worth every penny in my eyes. (Though I am sure my parents wouldn't agree.) By the time the fall semester of my Sophomore year rolled around, I was put on probation and told "...if (my) grades don't improve, (I) will be kicked out."

"You aren't smart enough and you will never amount to anything!" was my brain-stamped truth.

I flunked out of college.

I told all my friends and family that my parents could no longer pay for my schooling and that I would have to live at home and go to a local, less expensive school. Those who knew me then and are reading this now, are hearing this for the very first time. This has been a secret that I have been carrying for more than twenty-five years . . . and it's almost as many years since something changed in me.

Something told me I was worth more than those words that I had heard for so long . . . those words that already defined so much of my life and attempted to define my future being. I wish I could remember exactly what happened to cause the transformation. I'd love to tell you I read a book that spoke to me,

saw a quote that rang through my head, acquired a mentor who talked some sense into me, or saw a movie that pulled me out of this hole, but I can honestly say there is no one defining moment that sticks out in my mind. I do, however, remember meeting my gift of a husband who I have now known for more than twenty-six years, so maybe it was something he said or did.

Kim with her (now) husband, Nick.

To him, I was beautiful *and* smart.

I remember struggling internally when my (now) husband and I first started dating. I remember him supporting me through whatever I needed to do in order to be the full person he already believed I was.

I remember going to see a counselor, so maybe it was something that happened during those sessions that caused an internal change in me. I know that I very quickly made an intentional choice, after some purposeful reflection, to let go of almost four years of silent torment. I also chose not to blame, point fingers, ask for apologies, or go backward in time.

I believe in my heart of hearts that this boy has probably grown up to be a wonderful man and that this was just a period in his life of immaturity brought on by his own circumstances and secrets. I also believe that, if it wasn't for this experience in my life, I wouldn't be the strong person that I am today.

I continued to take courses at community colleges to find out who and what I was meant to be. I never failed a class again and in fact never got below a 3.0 GPA. Then, at the age of twenty-four, I found my gift and joy in real estate. I am today running the Keller Williams Milwaukee Southwest Market Center, leading over 130 real estate agents and staff.

'Take that, you-will-never-amount-to-anything-thinking, girl!'

It's funny how your mind controls everything. You're controlled by what you say to yourself, how you feel about yourself, how you carry yourself, the energy that you choose to walk around with daily - all of that crazy, inspirational, affirmation-filled, feel-good shit. Yes, I non-apologetically admit that I am one of those "glass is half full" kind of people. But, you know what?

It works!   *Confidence and laughter in a life worth living!*

Call me crazy or lucky or whatever, but experts agree that eighty to ninety percent of one's success is based on what we say to ourselves in our heads. I actually believe that it's closer to ninety-nine-point-nine percent! I am not a genius, but I can certainly recite one mean, mind-blowing, life-changing affirmation.

Sometimes, I remind myself that I can be both the pretty one and the smart one . . . even, occasionally the athletic one. But, my first affirmation of the morning is usually:

"Oh yeah! My hair is still pretty big and mean!"

"Follow your passion, it will

lead to your purpose."

~ Oprah Winfrey

EXPERIENCE

◆ ◆ ◆

An experience worth giving to others is one in which you share your authentic self, allowing your unique talents to shine for the success of others. Exceed expectations and add value by developing a deep bond of trust.

You build your own character through every experience, whether it is positive or negative. This is where you learn and grow. In failing, be sure to fail forward. Embrace it; roadblocks are an inevitable opportunity to pivot and reach for goals with a new and improved perspective. Use that perspective to offer the immeasurable gift of grace to others when they fail, and to yourself when you are struggling.

Change your mind set by believing in yourself, using positive affirmations, and removing limiting beliefs. The results will astound as you dig into new and noteworthy value-providing experiences.

◆　◆　◆

"Success is a journey not a destination. Enjoy the Journey."

~Brian Tracy

Jeremy Rynders has an entrepreneurial spirit and has been a successful realtor for the past ten years in the Milwaukee area. However, it's his prior life experiences with a family-owned dude ranch in Arizona that invoke a life lesson. We all have dreams and aspirations that pass us by, resulting in regret. We tend to limit ourselves from within because of fear of the unknown and we focus on what can go wrong. Instead, he wants readers to think about saying "yes" to an opportunity they might have in life or, even better, to be the ones that create the opportunities for others!

FAITH, DETERMINATION, AND NAIVETE

Jeremy Rynders

◆ ◆ ◆

"You'll come as guests and leave feeling like family."

T he question and answer in my story is both simple and complicated. Take a risk and say "yes" to an authentic once-in-a-lifetime opportunity? Say "no" and go on to the typical path of life that so many blindly accept and tolerate: job or college and career. Not that there's a right answer for all people, but there is a right one for each individual. What was mine?

Growing up as the middle child in an otherwise normal family of five, we always did one thing abnormally. Anytime we went on vacations (which was frequently), we always left the oldest sibling behind and traveled as a family of four. As a child, or even as a young adult, I didn't think much of it; there was a logical reason why we operated this way, which I'll explain later. However, what I didn't realize was how this concept would go on to shape the rest of mine and our family's lives forever. It is this concept of leaving one sibling behind for vacations, combined with my mom's aspirations, that drove her and my dad to alter the trajectory of our family's path from a typical life in the "burbs," to one that very few, if any, have traveled, or will ever travel.

This journey is rooted in 1969 when my mother, Carrie, was a ten-year-old city girl in Milwaukee reading a book series titled: *Trixie Belden* and one particular story, *Mystery in Arizona*, combined with her passion and love for horses stuck with her, not just in childhood, but into adulthood, too. The experience and memories she had reading this book about a dude ranch full of horses and adventure in Arizona would not go away. She felt compelled to not just daydream about it anymore, but instead make it a reality in our lives.

Fast forward to 1993 when the four of us: Carrie, my dad, Dan, my younger sister Vicki (age nine), and I (age thirteen) once again left my oldest sister Amy (age seventeen) back home to embark on our annual ten to fourteen-day summer vacation driving trip in the ol' conversion van. We knew this trip was going to be a completely different experience from our typical touristy driving trip to Mt. Rushmore, or Florida, or the Carolinas, as we were headed to a Dude Ranch in Colorado called the . . . *Bar Lazy J. A Dude Ranch?*

We knew of my mom's interest and moderate passion for horses over the years. We even owned a horse that we boarded off site and we kids rode occasionally around an arena, or in our subdivision full of houses, but that's about it. So why would we *all* go to a Dude Ranch in the mountains of Colorado?

When we arrived it was the definition of serenity: *the state of being calm, peaceful, and untroubled.* We fully expected to ride horses on this trip and maybe even see cattle like the movie *City Slickers* portrayed. Instead, I recall a few specific feelings that were both so unexpected and also so welcoming: the most basic was that they didn't have any locks anywhere – not even on our guest room door! *'What? How was that possible? This can't possibly be allowed, can it?'*

We asked why and they said, "That's the way it's always been at the ranch and it's never posed a problem." – you could tell they enjoyed getting asked this question over and over by "City Slickers" like us upon their arrival.

As kids, we quickly embraced this concept and thought it was really cool – there was something significant about this level of trust that was automatically granted to everyone who chose to stay there and it worked both ways. We could go into any common building or guest room and anyone could come into our room, too – wow this place was truly different than anywhere else we'd been!

Some other surprises at the ranch were: the sight and sounds of a nearby rushing river, nightly campfires and star gazing, no televisions to be found anywhere, all the ranch guests and ranch hands eating three meals together every day, and the ability to go outside at any time, day or night, to watch and listen to the pasture full of horses eating, running around, playing . . . or just being still. We all loved the family atmosphere, connection to nature, and the free spirit feeling we felt. Those happy surprises and feelings, combined with the experience of meeting and getting to know so many people from around the world made the dude ranch, simply put, a special place.

Vicki and I thought we were on just another family vacation, when in reality my parents were trying to decide if a "dude ranch life" would be everything they had envisioned, or something to run for the hills from! They quickly discovered during our visit that this was indeed something they wanted our family to pursue and, from my mom's perspective, the sooner the better.

For approximately the next four, years my parents dreamed, discussed, and planned ways to make this dream a reality. Finally, in 1998 the timing was right as my dad was fifteen years into his career and ready for a change in scenery (figuratively *and* literally). This trigger, combined with we kids now being old enough (kind of) to decide for ourselves to either embark on this journey with them and be significant contributors to the new family business or stay home and choose that traditional life path of a getting a "normal job" or going to college *followed by* a career (and student debt). Much to our surprise we realized they had been seriously considering this together for the past several years.

They approached Vicki (who was still a sophomore in high school) and I separately and asked if we would be interested in moving to Arizona as a family, building a new dude ranch in the middle of nowhere, and all living and working there together. What? Really? Selling our house that we recently built, abruptly saying goodbye to all our family and friends, and moving across the country to live on a dude ranch with mom and dad? Seriously? At nineteen years old, and one year into a boring accounting degree, plus the same steady girlfriend, Jodi, for the past four years, it was this moment in time when I faced the life altering decision of saying "yes" to a scary, but exciting, once-in-a-lifetime opportunity . . . or no.

Why was this decision not one that Amy had to choose. Why *did* we travel with only four of the five in our family, always leaving my oldest sister Amy behind on vacations? Amy has Cerebral Palsy, is mentally challenged, can barely walk or talk other than a few words and hand motions, and spends most of her life in a wheelchair. It was very difficult to bring her on family vacations because of accessibility issues at resorts, attractions, beaches, airplanes, etc. Dude ranches were no exception. It was even harder to create accessibility for "dudes" in wheelchairs because of the typical remote setting, rough terrain, and the very nature of horseback riding and old western lodges and buildings. As our family was contemplating a move to Arizona to build, as well as own and operate a dude ranch, accessibility became an obvious issue and, at the same time, an exciting problem to solve.

With such a big decision to make, we all decided it would be a good idea to take one more trip to another dude ranch. We wanted to make sure it was equally as enjoyable as *The Bar Lazy J* was to all of us many years earlier. This time, we'd visit a ranch in Arizona to jive with my mom's *Mystery in Arizona* story and to experience that terrain, climate, and southwestern setting versus the western one that Colorado and Wyoming ranches offered. We also wanted to actually bring Amy along this time to find out if she enjoyed being on a ranch or not.

Mom had been a travel agent for twelve years and was familiar with researching travel destinations. A mom's search for a dude ranch that would at least try to accommodate her disabled daughter had begun! Call after call after call was met with a similar response: "As much as we'd love to help you and your family, we simply don't have the proper equipment or accommodations that would work for your family, we're very sorry and we hope you find a different ranch that can help you."

Finally, Carrie talked to the owners of a ranch named the *Kay El Bar Dude Ranch* in Wickenburg, Arizona. The friendly and ambitious owners of this ranch said: "While we're certainly not equipped to handle a wheelchair guest like Amy, we're more than willing to try our best to accommodate and see what happens," and that is all my mom and dad needed to hear!

By the end of March of 1998, the decision had been made. All of us had agreed to say, "yes," including my girlfriend, Jodi, who agreed to come along. (She was basically family at that point, anyway). For my younger sister and I, our "yes' was not without hesitation or fear, or even a tad of resentment – especially from Vicki who had to leave her high school. I personally had more of a "cautiously optimistic" tone combined with a "you-only-live-once-so-why-the-heck-not" attitude toward the whole potential adventure and experience.

Shortly after we all returned from the *Kay El Bar*, one of my parents was reading the local newspaper, the Journal Sentinel. In what was surely a twist of fate, a gift from God, or whatever you want to call it, because—in April of

1998—there was an ad that read "Cheap land for sale in Arizona – 40 acre parcels for only $21,900!"

My parents immediately called the toll free number and a friendly realtor, Angie Hardy, answered the phone. That call led to my parents buying 160 acres in Yucca, Arizona!

Really?

Just like that we owned the rights to land in the *Stagecoach Trails* land development which was literally in the middle of nowhere in Northwest Arizona. They now had ninety days to go and view the land in person and either confirm the deal, or get their deposit fully refunded. On Memorial Day weekend, only one to two months after visiting the *Kay El Bar* (which was just an hour and a half south of our new land) my mom, dad, and younger sister went viewed the 160 acres they purchased sight unseen over the phone!

The realtor conveniently had a few four-wheeler quads available to tour the tens of thousands of surrounding acres owned by the State of Arizona. She wanted us to get a feel for the mountain ranges and what this area was like. The road (basically our driveway) to our land was eleven miles of rough, bumpy dirt.

They did not return with any of the deposit money and instead officially owned 160 acres in Arizona. I'm sure the word "unreal" (so strange as to appear imaginary; not seeming real) is about how I felt at that time.

Once the decision was made to go after this dream, the difficult part began. It's always easy to dream, but it is rarely easy to execute the dream in real life. Not only did we have to convince the bank we had a great idea so we could finance the project (no, we did not have a rich uncle or a large inheritance), but we also had to leave our very close-knit extended family, friends, and home in Wisconsin and start a whole new life along with a new business – yikes! With our strong and resourceful immediate family and God's help, we knew we could do it.

Carrie (my mom) wrote the business plan, did her own research, and knocked on many bank doors. We all knew someone else out there would believe in our family's concept of building a brand-new dude ranch that was accessible for all and would offer a therapeutic riding program for *anyone* who had the desire to ride a horse at a dude ranch. Finally, after months of phone calls and conversations with financial institutions, we found someone who was willing to finance the project. Derhaag put together a loan for us that would enable our accessible dude ranch to come true. He also helped us secure additional financing through another bank since they could only finance part of our loan. If it weren't for Gregory's faith in our family's dream, *Stagecoach Trails Guest Ranch* in Yucca, Arizona would've never been built.

We spent endless hours designing and creating the ranch with my uncle Randy (mom's brother . . . not rich, but rich in generosity); he was both an architectural designer and builder. My mom focused on the interior and design and dad and my uncle fixated on the exterior and functional design. We were very careful to ensure the accessibility of every building, guest room, pool, and exterior area like porches, courtyards, corrals, and even the paths to and from the fourteen different buildings.

Having personal experience with Amy, we knew we could put ourselves in the shoes of all of our guests and their families to create a place that truly was barrier free. We were also careful to create a dude ranch where the accessibility was subtle. We wanted all able-bodied guests to feel welcome as well. It was to be a dude ranch first and foremost . . . that just happened to be accessible for all! My uncle Randy spent a lot of time in Arizona with us during this process. The more he was there, the more he fell in love with it.

However great this dream was in our own minds, the journey in real life was not easy. There were many days of frustration, despair, worry, and doubts. In July of 1999, just days before we made the big move out west, we received a phone call from the bank that was financing our additional loan funds. They were pulling out for unknown reasons; we couldn't believe this was happening! My mom called Gregory in a panic because we were only days away from giving up everything and moving out west to start our new life. We felt our dream fading away quickly but he told me not to worry. He said: "make the move and he would find another bank!" We trusted him and so we sold our house, packed up our belongings, said goodbye to our family and friends, and made the 2,000-mile journey to Arizona. Within days, while still on the way driving our moving trucks to Arizona, Gregory (Dad) had found us another bank! We rented a home in nearby Lake Havasu City and began finalizing plans for building the ranch as soon as possible. If it weren't for Gregory's belief in our family's dream, *Stagecoach Trails Guest Ranch* would never have been built – at this point the determination of a complete stranger was the determining factor in our lives!

Just when we thought things were going well we hit another major stumbling block. Our general contractor doubled his original budget pricing three days before our construction loan closed. He blamed it on rising lumber costs - we blamed it on greed. My mom was heartbroken and I recall her sobbing as we all knew there was no way we could secure additional financing for the ranch. The bank would only finance so much and we were at our personal limit to contribute. If we called them now to tell them the prices had doubled, they would surely cancel the loan. The plan of building a dude ranch in Arizona was slowly turning back from reality into a dream again.

While my mom sat crying, I started re-working the numbers on paper.

Luckily, us "kids" had the right amount of faith, determination . . . and naivete.

We convinced and re-motivated our parents to find a new contractor who would be willing to build the ranch at a price we could afford. We also made another decision that night. Because God gave us so many creative and construction talents, we realized we had better use them! By contributing to the contruction efforts, we knew we could afford to build the ranch. We simply had to do more of the work ourselves, but the great thing was, we were capable of it. Within days, we had another general contractor secured and we were on our way once again to building *Stagecoach Trails Guest Ranch*!

Finally, after years of planning, moving, and constantly thinking about this ranch, we now began to actually build it. We had professionals who did all the big stuff like framing, electrical, plumbing, drywall, stucco and roofing. However, there were so many other aspects and little things that we did ourselves. We lived and breathed building the ranch every day, all day. By "we," I'm also meaning both my grandma and grandpa from my dad's side and my Uncle Randy, along with his wife and teenage son. All of them felt compelled to move out to Arizona full-time to help us get the ranch built. We bought a thirty-year-old, rickety travel trailer to keep onsite and live in as opposed to driving an hour back and forth to Lake Havasu City on most nights.

Dad bought a large, used yellow Ford tractor and some survey equipment. This allowed my dad, grandpa and I to do all the grading and preparation of the soil for ten building foundations. We dug endless trenches for conduit and piping. We tiled the floors, installed finish trim, put in the wood floors, fencing, and corrals, set up the tack room, landscaped, painted, decorated, added lighting, completed a commercial kitchen install, and built—start to finish—our two 1,200 square foot personal residences that were on site.

The ranch resulted from countless hours of determination and hard work by each family member. In less than nine months, mostly during the daunting, Arizona summer heat, we built all ten buildings including: a large lodge, dining room, commercial kitchen, two buildings with a total of ten guest rooms, two small guest houses, two personal residences, pool and hot tub, workers' quarters, tack room, corral, and saddling area.

Upon completion, we named it *Stagecoach Trails Guest Ranch.*

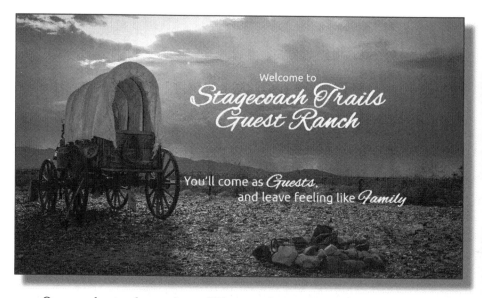

Our ranch stood proud on 320 acres in northwestern Arizona. It was located between Lake Havasu City and Kingman, Arizona – about two hours south of Las Vegas. The nearby land had remained relatively untouched and still looked like the true "Wild West." The ranch was surrounded by three separate mountain ranges and adjoined to approximately 360,000 acres of untouched Federal and State land. Our riding opportunities were virtually endless and offered expansive 360 views for miles. All of the fourteen guest rooms were spacious and handicapped accessible and the swimming pool and hot tub had a chair lift so disabled guests could use them too. Wheelchairs could go anywhere at the ranch, including the beautiful western lodge where guests could hang out. There was a southwestern style dining room and a large courtyard in between-all with beautiful mountain, desert, sunrise, and sunset views.

Miraculously (it was literally a miracle), *Stagecoach Trails Guest Ranch* opened its doors on December 6th, 2000! Our first and only guests that week was a film crew from England – yes, we filmed a TV show before we ever had a single paying guest check in! One of the most interesting parts of their trip was that we had purchased four two-seater go-karts for them to enjoy that had no suspensions and were built for street and minor off-road use only. We wanted to impress them as much as we could, so we used the go-karts to trek into the nearby mountain ranges and the long trail we used was unbelievably rugged. Wow, that trip was a minor disaster and of course they thought it was awesome and loads of fun! Luckily the host of the TV show was adventurous, and the main feature of the show was a teenage boy in a wheelchair along with is older brother. They loved everything about the ranch including the crazy go-kart ride, the accessibility of the ranch and the disabled riding program we offered. This resulted in our episode receiving a lot of attention in the U.K. and we quickly had a lot of guests coming from England. Several months later we hosted another English film crew who also did a story about us. This time the host was in a wheelchair and they loved it so much they did an even larger feature story about us which brought even more attention throughout Europe and subsequently many more European guests! This was yet another example of something we never could've planned or counted on – things just happened to fall into place.

The first several months of being open were extremely difficult as we had only a few guests and lots of bills to pay. Being a new dude ranch in an era of brochures, word-of-mouth advertising, and card racks at gas stations and welcome centers made it almost impossible to start immediately with paying guests. We spent a lot of time wondering about that phrase "if you build it they will come!" and kept thinking, *'maybe they don't come if you build it in the middle of nowhere!'* Luckily for us a few more things fell into place: a) satellite internet for small businesses had just become readily available so we were able to get online within months of opening, b) by the year 2000, the internet was becoming mainstream and the travel industry was one of the earliest benefactors, and c) as a result of our "trial by fire," I figured out how to build our website, design our brochures, and market the new ranch all over the world. Between the internet and the TV show, we gradually gained popularity and soon had guests coming from all over the world.

Another unpredictable factor in our success was the exchange rate for different currencies from around the globe – something we never thought about before. It turned out the British Pound and Euro were very strong at this time – guests using the British Pound could visit the USA for basically half price! This, combined with their love of old western movies meant experiencing dude ranches in America as a very popular holiday for them. We had many guests visit us over and over and over again – they could not get enough. Some came all the way from Europe twice in the same year and would stay for two weeks at a time! Our closeness to Las Vegas and the Grand Canyon certainly helped, too.

While we felt it, we initially didn't know for sure that one of the biggest factors in our future success would be our motto: *"You'll come as guests and leave feeling like family."* This set the tone and expectations for our family, staff, and guests. I believe this simple phrase allowed our guests to book their trip and arrive with a different mindset – they came *expecting* to leave a few days or weeks later feeling like family. We all felt obligated to fulfill that expectation and this positive hospitality resulted in overwhelming success. A by-product of us delivering on this promise was that our guests felt compelled to write long passionate reviews on websites like tripadvisor.com – the most popular travel research and review website in the world. This, in turn, fed our popularity and future success. We even won multiple awards from Trip Advisor for the amount of reviews and high ratings we had – wow!

Our ranch, one that was accessible for anyone, went on to be very successful in many different ways. We had an outstanding riding program for

Amy poses with her mom and dad

both able-bodied and disabled riders. We had a wheelchair ramp and two-sided platform so helpers could stand firmly on both sides of the horse and rider. This enabled all our disabled guests the opportunity to safely get on, and back off the horse. This could be a very challenging and dangerous process depending on their ability to control their body and how flexible they were. The horses we used for this program were well-trained and used to sporadic movements by the riders (some had uncontrollable muscle spasms, too). However, there was always a chance a horse could "freak out." We did have a few scary moments over the years, but thankfully nothing serious.

The concept of therapeutic riding has gained popularity around the world. It's a great way for those who cannot walk to feel that sensation of walking, either again, or for the first time in their life – it can be a magical thing! Depending on the comfort level of the rider and his or her sense of adventure, we either took the disabled rider in the round arena, or out on the miles and miles of trails. We provided side-walkers for a safe and memorable ride. Our family and staff would spend hours and hours walking alongside the horses to hold the riders' legs while navigating the hilly, rocky terrain and the cacti. This allowed people who had never walked on their own two feet or ridden a horse outside of an arena, to experience a real trail ride like they had dreamed about. Their family members could be on horseback and go along on the rides, too. This really made for a memorable experience for our disabled guests and their families.

Our abled bodied riding program was just as popular. Most dude ranches only allowed walking on trails, or a very limited amount of trotting and loping in short areas. Because we allowed qualified guests to actually trot and lope thru the desert washes (dry sandy rivers) for long distances, our riding program was a real hit with our guests. We also frequently offered half- and full-day rides with spectacular views and challenging terrains deep into the mountains with our entertaining wranglers.

After all of our trials and tribulations, the many reasons why it wouldn't work, and natural obstacles that should've prevented this from happening, our ranch family went on to host over 25,000 guests! It was a total family effort with us all working day and night, seven days-a-week, anytime the ranch was open . . . which was about eleven months out of the year. I became a full time jack of all trades and did everything around the ranch. This included doing dishes for our three meals per day, to cleaning guest rooms, to feeding horses, to being an ATV trail guide, to pool boy, webmaster, marketing manager, and even part of the nightly entertainment.

About nine months after the ranch opened Jodi and I got married at the ages of twenty-one and twenty, respectively. We lived and worked at the ranch together for about nine years and, after the birth of our first child, Sophie, we decided to move back to Wisconsin in June of 2008.

The Stagecoach Trails Guest Ranch was my home, work, and passion for almost ten years. Saying "yes" to that chapter of my life taught me many life lessons around grit, family, construction, hospitality, and small-business skills. I truly experienced hard work, dedication, creative innovation, and the value of establishing quality experiences for others. Over my years there, in addition to thousands of international travelers, I was able to see hundreds of people like

Amy find joy on horseback in ways that they never imagined would be available to them. The fulfillment of being a part of that can't be understated.

Jeremy and other staff on a sunset ride in Arizona.

After leaving the ranch, Jodi and I hopped into that *typical* life together. We left Mom, Dad, and a well-loved, familial staff to continue to run the ranch. My parents went on owning and operating the ranch through July of 2014 when they sold it and handed the reins over to a new ranch family. My parents sold *Stagecoach Trails* so they could move back to Wisconsin. They wanted to be back with family, friends, and especially their grandchildren, since Jodi and I, as well as Vicki and her family, had all moved back to Wisconsin.

Today Jodi and I have three daughters and we happily work in real estate through both sales and owning and managing investment properties. Through real estate and our Keller Williams office, I like to think I'm still trying to establish quality experiences for others. There is no doubt that my success in real estate is directly related to my saying "yes," as a nineteen-year-old kid, to that once-in-a-lifetime opportunity. That kid went off to discover that the true "Mystery in Arizona" was that a dedicated group people with the right faith, determination, (and maybe naivete) could make an idea come to life . . . to begin making a difference in the lives of others.

◆　◆　◆

"The pain that you

experience in life shouldn't

make you look down on

yourself."

~ *Dodinsky*

Michelle Mueller has been in an Accounting profession for fifteen years. She is CFO for the Keller Williams, Milwaukee Southwest office and she leads that market center, with six others. She is eager to come to work every day and enjoys being part of the largest growing real estate business in the area. Michelle resides in Big Bend, Wisconsin with her husband, Mike and children, Lauren and Michael. She has a passion for cooking, fishing, party planning, and outdoor living and is also involved in her kids' extracurricular activities in both sports and music. Her Big Why: "To provide tools, encouragement, and support, so that those I've encountered have been influenced by inspiration, value, and knowledge, while creating a personal story of fulfillment and success!"

SANITIZED

Michelle Mueller

The air was stale with smells of disinfectant, bandages, cotton balls, alcohol wipes, and needles; it was *complete* sterilization. The sounds of adjustable beds, IVs, monitors, code calls over the intercom, beeping noises, rolling carts, and the clicks of computers filled that stale air. The memories and sounds of complete and utter chaos came back to me as I turned my head one last time to say "goodbye" to rooms 12 and 3553. This would be the start of a new journey and one of uncertainty. One thing that *was* certain to me; this was a place I never wanted to visit again!

◆　◆　◆

It was a typical winter, weekday morning. Snow was on the ground, like any other January day. The air was fresh and the sun was shining; not a cloud in the sky. The kids and I woke up at our normal time, packing lunches and getting ready with our daily routine. We said our goodbyes at the bus stop and off to work and school we went. This was a usual workday for me, repetitive and uneventful, until 11:00 A.M. when my stomach started to feel upset. I was sure this was hunger pangs and thought it would be a good idea to warm up a can of chicken noodle soup. I began to take a bite and made the decision that this feeling was not the result of hunger. I told my coworkers, it might be best if I left for the day to rest; I would see them tomorrow.

Little did my colleagues and I know, we would not be reunited for more than five weeks. I arrived home and thought it was in my best interest to call my mom who lived just two houses away. After all, she had been a nurse for fifty years and would be able to give me medical advice on what the next steps should be for me. She greeted me in my living room, on the couch, laying with my favorite down-filled blanket wrapped around me.

I *couldn't* get comfortable; the pain would not subside; I asked, "What should I do?"

A decision to visit Urgent Care followed; it was just a random stomach ache, right? Unfortunately, I knew something felt "different" about this. I was taken from the Urgent Care room in a wheelchair, to the attached Emergency facility. Test after test was performed! *'What was going on? What was happening to me? I just have a stomach ache, don't I? Wasn't this just a flu bug?'*

I was being told what was happening, but wasn't comprehending any of it. The pain in my stomach was worsening with every passing moment! Suddenly, two men arrived from out of the blue, wanting to transfer me from the ER bed, onto a stretcher. *'Where was I going?'* I was told that the need to rush me to the hospital . . . was great. *'What was happening?'*

I still didn't understand and I started to black out from the intense pain. A sad "goodbye" followed with my mom, who had stayed in the ER with me, from the time I arrived. She needed to get my children, which was the most important thing at that time. They needed to know I was sick and would not be home. She assured me the kids would be taken care of – Michael, then six, and Lauren, thirteen. I was going . . . *alone* . . . to the hospital via ambulance. I was scared, but strong.

My husband, Mike, worked third shift and, many times, into the daylight hours, so he was not home when this was happening. When my mom left the Emergency Room, she called and told him things were more severe than expected. I was getting a stomach ache checked out at the Urgent Care, which now was turning into an ambulance ride to Waukesha Memorial Hospital. When we arrived, I was admitted and immediately rushed from a medical-surgical room, into Intensive Care (room 12). I still had no idea what was happening! *'SOMEONE, please tell me what is happening to me!'*

I started to close my eyes, as if trying to make this nightmare go away. Those eyes would remain closed for days, avoiding the reality of what was happening before them. What was about to happen next, would put the strongest, most faith-driven individual, through the biggest challenge of her life.

"God is my strength and defense."
~Exodus 15:1-4

An immediate CT scan in radiology determined a diagnosis; pancreatitis: an attack of the pancreas, in which the organ starts to eat itself and will continue to do so until death occurs. A blood test revealed a triglyceride measurement of 5000 when normal levels should be below 100. Time was of the essence!

I knew things were bad when Mike ran out the door crying, torn up; he couldn't bear to watch his wife go through this.

A port was quickly stuck into the main artery of my neck, with what seemed to be an inches long device. Tubes were shoved down the nose, into the throat, past the gag reflex, and into the stomach, drawing out the poison that was running through my body. They had to stop the destruction of the Pancreas, before it was too late! Blood draw . . . after blood draw . . . after blood draw. A catheter was shoved in (later determined to have been done for no reaason) and I have immediate denial of any drink or food.

Crying.

Pain

Sreaming.

Yelling.

Staff member after staff member was not allowing me a single *minute* to breath and absorb all of the painful things they were doing to me!

"Will she die?" I hear Mike ask the doctors, plural. (I had now been assigned to a team of ten medical professionals in control of my destiny).

"We don't know," one said.

Power of Attorney paperwork followed and was urgently signed, proving how sick I really was.

Mike lost it and was consoled by the team of medical professionals.

'Why, when I was eighteen and told I had high Triglycerides, did I not think this was serious? Why, when the Triglycerides kept rising with age, and the doctors told me I was now at risk for Pancreatitis, did I not comprehend how serious this lipid disorder, really was?' Yes, I had a genetic disorder, detected very young in life, affecting the cholesterol makeup in my body. *'Why,*

why, why, did this horrible event have to happen to me?' No one was explaining what they were doing to me.

I was in HELL and was not sure I was making it out alive!

I couldn't talk; I had no water; my tongue stuck to the roof of my mouth. I was so thirsty and, for the next seven days, the ability to drink was ripped away from me. I could definitely relate to the story of Lazarus and the Rich Man (Luke 16:19-31).

The poison, secreting from the Pancreas, had to be excreted by the tube shoved so vigorously down my nose and throat. It was still burning and making me sick to my stomach, as a result of being shoved down with no warning! I was gagging every second and could not bear this tube. I was denied water, over and over. My husband begged for me to get some liquid, as he watched me, unable to speak. My Pancreas was so sick and damaged, it was not able to process *anything* consumed by mouth! I was so sad and couldn't think about anyone but myself. The mother, who had worried every second in the past about her children's whereabouts and well-being, who put everything and everyone before herself, was no longer able to think about anything but fighting for her life! *'Or, did I? Did I really want to fight for my life? I was in a nightmare, brought to that life!'*

My triglyceride level could only be fixed by one, long, three-hour process called "Plasmapheresis." This was a procedure where all of the plasma running through my body, now a deep "pink" in color and as thick as Milk of Magnesia, was replaced with healthy, non-poisonous plasma. They actually replaced my blood.

From the bottom of my heart, "Thank you," to the fifty-six individuals, who donated blood to help reduce my Triglyceride levels by 4100 to a new level of 900!

But this new marker of 900 was not enough, for my team of ten. I was still at very high risk and was told I needed to repeat the Plasmapheresis procedure again! After another three-hour process, with the help of another fifty-six donors, my new Triglyceride level reveals, 400! Unbeknownst to over 100 people, they saved my life!

My pancreas had been stopped from destroying itself and healthy plasma relieved my body from working so hard.

Unfortunately, I was not out of the woods yet. Even though my Triglyceride levels had tapered off, the pancreas was still draining poison, into this clear container, behind my hospital bed. The liquid was green and black and looked like tar! *'This is coming from my body?'* Until that container stopped filling up, there was no way I was going to be allowed drink for a very long time. The inability to quench my thirst or sleep, due to the intense pain, was affecting me emotionally.

After three days without any water, a kind nurse, gave me a sugar free candy to suck on. The feeling of that lozenge in my mouth, made my entire day, month, week! My mouth, now less dry and able to talk, was experiencing an amazing sensation. It's easy to take everyday life for granted when one tiny act of kindness, can impact a person's entire being.

It had been five days in the hospital. I hadn't slept for more than one hour at a time. My body, though healing, was becoming weaker and weaker. The rooms were dark; I felt my Vitamin D draining from my body. I didn't know if it was sunny, rainy, snowy, or cold. I asked to take walks, knowing this would be the most difficult task for me, but necessary. The staff was so busy, I was lucky to get one walk per day. After all, most patients in ICU, don't actually have the ability to go for walks. Watching my husband, day after day, sleep in a hospital chair, never to leave my side, made me want to get better, even more. I had no control over this. I was at God's mercy.

"Strengthen me according to your word."
~Psalm 119:28

Finally, the day arrived when that black and green goo I called tar, was no longer collecting in that container behind me. My Pancreas had taken another step in the healing process and I was allowed to drink, for the first time in seven days! I felt like a kid in a candy store! Something as simple as a drink of water, had gained more appreciation and reverence, than I ever imagined. I will cherish the feel of water from a cold glass as it hits my tongue for the rest of my life. I was so grateful for something so small. My body was able to digest and I handled those first drinks well. What followed, was sherbet and yogurt, also tolerated. I had passed the test in ICU and was able to transfer to a "med-surg" unit, with the intent to go home . . . *someday*.

I was settled into my new room (room 3553), eight long days after I was first admitted. It was getting harder and harder for all involved and I started to wonder if I would ever go home. My children had a hard time visiting me. I looked very sick and the tubes, IVs, and other signs of my battle scared them.

This made them sad and they would not come close to me. After all, mom had never been sick before. The kids watched me from afar and I could feel their empathy and pity for mom They were really starting to miss me at home, so my drive to get there grew fiercely!

Five more days passed in the medical-surgical unit and I was finally released to home. I was discharged in January, 2016, from Waukesha Memorial Hospital, with twelve prescriptions and completely Insulin-dependent. I had to take three daily pills, two of them vitamins, prior to this illness. I couldn't believe that I now needed a pill container to fit all of my new prescriptions.

'What has just happened to me,' I thought.

Home was the only other thing I could think about. I had to try and be a mother to my children again, but—at the same time—I didn't know how I was going to take care of myself. I hurt tremendously and wondered if I would ever be the same again. This was sure to be the beginning of a very rough journey for me.

After thirteen days, I was back at home. I had run up the sixteen steps to my main living area time and time again and, without thinking, thought I could run them like before! My body felt like fifty-pound weights were locked onto my ankles, weighing me down, more and more with each step. I made it up three and crawled the other thirteen.

I was weak and still in so much pain.

I couldn't sleep in my bed.

I couldn't breathe lying flat.

I couldn't bear the pain laying on my side.

All of my organs had been affected by Pancreatitis and the pain was almost unbearable. My stomach couldn't be touched, bumped, or even shifted wrong. Over the next three weeks, I slept in a chair, sitting upright, my legs on the coffee table, and my head propped by a pillow. It was the only way to breathe and alleviate some of the pressure in my stomach, from organs pressing up against one another, causing extreme pain.

I was hopeful I would eventually be on my way to recovery (mom always said give it a full six weeks from when you have any procedure or illness). My only activity for weeks was simply getting through a shower. I would look in the mirror and realize how genuinely sick and tired I looked. I had no color, my iron was low, my skin was pale, a huge gaping hole was in my neck from the port they put through it *('how would I ever hide this, it was huge')*, intense bruising was on my arms from repeat blood work, and sticky matter was all over, left behind from the medical tape; it would take a dozen showers to remove the glue!

I was forty-years old and looked over fifty. I knew it was going to take time to recover from this. I thought I would never get better; the doctors had wanted me to go back to work two days after discharge. '*WHAT were they thinking, when I couldn't even take a shower without help?'*

I was one of the toughest women I knew and there was no way I could drive myself to work, let alone make it through an entire day at my desk job. It was week five when I tried to lay on my side in bed – a task I had tried many times over and failed. For the first time, I didn't feel like I was going to fly through the roof from pain. This was followed by making it through the day without a nap, and then I was able to shower and get ready on my own, without help.

At the start of week six, I decided I would return to work to try to lead a normal life again. But, this was not the end for me. What I was about to endure would be some of the worst to come!

On my sixth week since diagnosis of Pancreatitis, other symptoms (the aftermath) started to reveal themselves. I started to lose my hair, as if going through chemotherapy. Chunks and chunks of hair were falling out, clogging the shower drain, with every washing. Trips to the hair salon followed; the need for my hair to be cut every week, shorter and shorter, so not to be obvious. My body had been through so much trauma that, until I was back to good health, I would not stop losing hair or start re-growing new hair . . . words straight from my hair stylist.

It was now seven weeks since diagnosis and I started to experience night sweats and tremors. Out of all of the things happening to me, this was the icing on the cake. I had no control over what was happening. I would wake up night after night with what I now know as panic attacks, accompanied by tremors, that I could not get rid of on my own. I would get on the treadmill at 2:00 A.M. to see if they would go away. I was told that panic attacks could be controlled by exercise. I walked miles and miles on the treadmill and usually, the attacks would go away on their own . . . until the next episode.

During this time, I had called my primary doctor and asked, "What can I do? These are happening in the midst of dead sleep and I don't know what can make them go away."

She immediately put me on a pill that increased serotonin in my body, a pill that would take weeks to start working. She offered nothing else for immediate relief. *'What was I supposed to do in the meantime?'*

I was still experiencing panic attacks and, at the times when I felt most relaxed, and I had no rescue medicine – nothing for immediate relief. What Doctor G didn't tell me was that this would be the most intense medication for your body to adjust to. The side effects were terrible and, although eventually helpful, it extremely difficult to surpass the serotonin building up in my system. *'Why would I ever want to put another one of these pills in my mouth? I knew that I had to give this pill time, but what could I do in the meantime?'*

That night (I had only been on the medication for four days), I had the worst attack of my life! I woke up, again from a dead sleep! My heart rate at 160 beats per minute, my nervous system, firing over and over and over again! My whole body felt like lightning was running through every vein, every artery, every organ! I felt like I was being electrocuted over and over again. I got on my treadmill and ran six miles. I had never been able to exceed two miles before!

I needed this to end, *'OH, dear LORD help me!'*

I was experiencing a nervous breakdown and wanted to die! I couldn't stop the pain and I prayed and prayed to God, asking for help. I was sure He was listening, but the time wasn't right for Him to step in. I called my doctor in the middle of the night; my husband's company hired private doctors; this was one of the benefits. I told her what was going on. My mom had told me to ask for something more immediate. I needed a medicine to help me now, not in one month, when the pill with the serotonin, would finally start working.

She denied me; she told me, that I needed to wait for the pill to work as it would help eventually. I mentioned what my mom had told me and she said, "I AM NOT GIVING YOU ANY XANAX OR VALIUM, THAT YOU COULD ABUSE! YOU'RE NOT GETTING THAT FROM ME!"

I had never taken any rescue drug like this before. I didn't even know the names of the drugs she was talking about! All I knew was I needed help to stop these tremors and the nervous system from firing over and over. I wanted to die and asked God to take it all away.

'Why wouldn't this doctor help me?' This would be something I couldn't forgive her for, for a very long time. Dr. G ended up referring me to a clinic that specialized in panic and tremor disorders. Again, though, her tone was very heartless and unsupportive. With her lack of emotion, she said, "It will probably take six weeks for you to get an appointment."

Obviously, this doctor trusted no one, not even her own patients. I called and left a message with this clinic to call back. I couldn't work; I couldn't exist in this world; I couldn't cope with what was happening to my body. I didn't know if I could go on.

'Why wasn't God helping me? I had never felt this way before and why (after five weeks off work and income and in a hospital, was I now going through the worst health challenge of my life) did He put more stress and health challenges on me?' I thought I had been through enough, but His purpose was far greater for me; I just had no idea what that was!

I wasn't able to sleep, to sit, to relax. I was in my kitchen alone looking out the window, at the snow, not sure what to do next. Experiencing a panic attack is truly the worst experience of one's life. My nervous system was still firing and my entire body trembled. My mom had spent the night with me and there was nothing she could do to help. She left and the only thought I had was that I wanted to die!

As a person of strong faith, I knew that only one person was allowed to take another's life, and that was God alone. I didn't care. Yes, one can actually feel so awful that life is no longer relevant. The intense breakdown was something I could not deal with another minute and surely not the weeks I was told it would take to get me into an appointment to help me get better. I stood there and thought, *'What would my poor family do without me, but how can I live this way another minute?'*

By some crazy act of faith, my mother-in-law's words came to mind. When I had questioned something this extreme before (my sister was going through Cancer and I wondered how could God put this family through this), she told me the question was not, "Why is God allowing this?" The question was, "How are you going to fight this Devil, that is winning with you?"

This was not God's work in progress!

This was the devil with a power so strong, he was weaseling his way into my heart when I was at the lowest point in my life! It was God helping me remember this and at the top of my lungs, I found myself screaming, "DEVIL, GET OUT OF MY LIFE!!!,YOU WILL NEVER WIN, MY HEART AND

SOUL ARE WITH GOD, SO GET THE HELL OUT, YOU WILL NOT WIN!!!!"

It was now ME, at the palm of his fiery hands; it was a place I had never been before and he almost won me over!

"My strength is perfect in weakness."
~Corinthians 12:9-10

Five minutes passed after this crazy episode in my kitchen, when my cell phone rang. It was the office, calling back, to help schedule an appointment with the specialty clinic. I explain my story telling them how I was trembling and what I am going through. I explained that what I felt was a nervous breakdown even more aggressive than a panic attack. I explained that I had never experienced anything like this before.

They were able to get me in, the *next* day!

It was a true miracle.

I was not only able to get into an appointment less than twenty-four hours later, I was able to have a kind-hearted, sensitive ear listening, and I mean truly listening, to my story – a person who cared and wanted to help me was on the other line. Indeed, it was God who stepped in (once He knew I would not forsake Him), to get me the help I needed. A short visit to this doctor determined that my serotonin was indeed low; I was given something for immediate help (after Dr G allowed me to suffer for so long that it ended with a nervous breakdown). The aftermath of Pancreatitis was brutal, but I was hopeful this would be a turning point for me, in the right direction.

"Through him who gives me strength."
~Phillipians 4:11-13

As time passed, my health was improving and I was getting back to my old self. And through this time, where death kissed me in the face, I realized how much more I had to offer this world. I sat at a desk for thirteen years in a position that would go nowhere. There were no growth opportunities, no opportunity to bring value to others, no rewards, and nowhere to go. I had been doing the same thing for thirteen years and was surrounded by a management team that was unsupportive, judgmental, and belittling, with no desire to help build wealth or a legacy for their employees.

I knew I needed to do more, to help others, to lead, to teach! I often thought, '*Who would have really remembered me, had I died? Would anyone, besides my immediate family, really miss me? What would I leave behind that would stand out as being amazing, accomplished, and purposeful?*'

I didn't feel the need to leave this world, honored as if Mother Theresa, but I wanted to know people would remember me for doing good, changing lives for the better, and being the supporter of others. I dreamed of being that well-loved person someday. I wanted to share all of the knowledge I had gained in the past twenty years of my working life. I was better than a desk job and knew I had so much more to offer.

I needed change and the prayers continued, every cool, breezy morning, that the spring months offered. I would pray in the parking lot of work. Before starting every single day, I asked God, "please bring opportunity my way. I don't need a lot God, but I know I have so much more to offer and I ask you lead me to that place."

I wanted a profession that would showcase my skills and through which, in turn, I could bring value to others. These prayers continued for months and months. I knew God was listening, but again, the time wasn't right to step in – until a late March, early spring evening. Snow was starting to melt and the summer months were coming closer. The family and I finished supper, and my phone rang. I didn't recognize the number, but answered. It was a call that would change my life, forever..

Scott Klaas, owner of a local and very new Keller Williams Real Estate Company in the area, called me on my cell phone, wanting to discuss a business opportunity which he had at his franchise. Scott, his business partner Jeremy, and I had worked together for three years at the job I was currently at. We had a very good working relationship and, when they needed an MCA (or what most people would call a CFO), it was my name that came to mind.

I might be a good "fit" for their company, he told me. It was an opportunity for me to become the Chief Financial Officer of Keller Williams, Milwaukee Southwest. Conversation after conversation and meeting after meeting concluded I would be the first and only Market Center Administrator, to help build, manage, and financially lead this business to success!

With reservation, I accepted the job and became a full-time employee on May 1st 2017. I was stepping out of my comfort zone, but everything about our meetings felt right and God indeed was stepping in, and leading me (again) to a new venture in my life. With hard work, dedication and the ability to believe in yourself, and put your trust wholeheartedly in the Lord, you can do anything! This sounds crazy and uncomfortable, but true. You don't have to settle for less, and you deserve to dream BIG! Don't let limiting beliefs allow you to settle for a dead-end job that does not showcase your God-given talent – one that does not allow you to believe in yourself and live out your life goals, to your full potential.

Indeed, I have a life to live, one which is worth living every day, because I have so much more to give this world, the agents in my market center, my amazing leadership team, and the amazing owner who brought me to believe in myself, to push myself as much (if not more) as I was pushed through horrible health issues. Supporting, empowering, and providing value through words and actions is what sets this owner's mindset above all others. Businesses succeed when those in charge want others to succeed. When your model is not to work against each other, but *for* each other, it will only thrive, because people want to be part of that awesome energy that one can feel the minute they walk into the office. I am blessed to be part of an amazing team of people, I love coming to work every day, and I thank God that this company has become part of my life, forever!

I'm sorry that Pancreatitis affected my life. I'm sorry that I didn't have enough money (it was $600.00 per month at the time) to take the medicine required to avoid this. I am sorry that I didn't have enough self-worth to take care of myself, the person everyone in my family counted on most. I made a huge mistake, one that could have resulted in death.

After all, what good am I to my loved ones, if I am not here? The food on the table and the gas in the car, was a far lesser need than the health of the mother and wife that everyone was fearful of losing. Thankfully, God's love is unconditional. He does not judge and does not have a cap on how much He supports, helps and forgives us. His love to His children is endless, and He will never forsake us for making poor decisions.

There is an oft-quoted and not-Biblical saying that "God does not give you more than you can handle". That is not true. In fact, He *does* give you more than you can handle, so that you have to turn to Him. It's how you deal with it that matters.

Michelle healthy with her family.

My journey was surely a testament of how far one can be pushed and how much I didn't put my life completely in His hands to be taken care of. That day will never be forgotten, but I know now that I will never, if even for a moment, allow the devil to step foot into my home or my life again! I know there is a place in Heaven for me, do you?

"So do not fear, for I am with you; do not be dismayed, for I am your God"
~Isaiah 41:10

I will never miss the year of Hell I went through, but from tragedy, came personal reflection, personal discovery, and self-worth. I knew I wanted to do more with my life! And if this is your dream, dig deep into your heart to find your strengths and your talent. Don't limit your beliefs to think your purpose is not there. Once you know your talents, search to find the path in life that makes you happy. Don't let yourself stay at a job which affects your health negatively, or surrounded by those who don't allow you to believe that you are worth so much more than sitting at a desk job five days a week with an opinion that never matters! (Unless *your* desk job *does* fulfill your purpose!) Don't be in a job that is never going to reveal an opportunity for you to grow. A true leader and owner will want you to be as successful as he or she is and will do everything to empower you to reach your goals. Your life and purpose are out there! Now go find them! Don't be fearful of change! Change is good and, if you just believe in yourself, you *can* accomplish anything.

Thank you, God for showing me that I cannot live my life without You, for saving me several times ,and for guiding me to come back to You when I was starting to leave. Thank you, Rooms 12 and 3553 for showing me what huge potential lied ahead. For showing me, that out of pain, can come growth and a true understanding of who you are and who you want to become. Thank you for revealing a life sanitized from meaninglessness.

"For I know the plans I have for you, "declares the LORD", plans to prosper you and not to harm you, plans to give you hope and a future."
~Jeremiah 29: 11

◆ ◆ ◆

"No pressure –

No diamonds."

~ kw MAPS BOLD LAWS

LEGACY

◆ ◆ ◆

A thought turns into an idea, turns into a dream.
It sets a fire inside of your soul.
It is your passion.
You are obsessed with planning it, seeing it
through, and fulfilling it.
It answers the question: "What is my purpose?"
You believe in it to the core of you being. You
advocate for it and have a one hundred percent
commitment to making it happen. The dream
becomes reality and grows stronger over time.

Mission accomplished.

Your passion creates curiosity and attracts
energy among others around you. You cast your
vision, ownership is taken, and the mission
continues on in a life of its own. It serves others
at a high level. Exponentially, it changes lives.

That is a true Legacy Worth Leaving.

◆　◆　◆

"People don't buy what you do; they buy why you do it, and what you do proves what you believe."

~ Simon Sinek

Jill LeCount is a devoted Wife, Mother, and Grandma (Naamah) who resides in southeastern Wisconsin. She graduated from Purdue University with a Bachelor of Science degree in nursing and currently holds a real estate broker's license. She is the co-founder of LeCount Realty—a division of Keller Williams—with her husband Steve. Jill loves to sell lakefront and rural properties. Her passion is spending time with her family while enjoying watersports. As a lifelong dog lover, Jill frequently takes long walks in the park with her German Shepherd, Jax. Jill's mission in life is to serve others with compassion, integrit,y and gratitude.

AN OCEAN OF LOVE

Jill LeCount

◆ ◆ ◆

E veryone has it.
Everyone longs for it.
All you need to do is just . . . *Go There!*

It's that special place where all of life just seems to make sense. The past, present, and future merge to provide the clarity and answers of our deepest and most difficult questions. Let me take you to my special place.

As I breathe in the salty air while the sun darkens my pale skin, I feel as though I could walk for miles and never tire. The sand between my toes washes away yet again with the coolness of the next wave. The pelicans soar the crest of the wave in search of their next meal. The sound of the crashing water engulfs my soul as it drowns out the worries of the day. The never-ending pattern of one wave after the other reminds me of the magnificence and power of our Almighty Creator. From the uniqueness of every seashell on the endless sandy beach, to the expanse of water before me, I am reminded of those who have shaped the woman I am today. The roaring waves help me to reflect on my life and the impact of those who have molded me. Although I've lived a life of contradictions: peacefulness and turmoil, sadness and awe – it is this place that grounds me and helps me to appreciate those I admire most while finding my true self.

From my earliest memories, my happiest times were those spent at the ocean. Although I don't remember it, I celebrated my first birthday at this huge puddle of water under the Florida sun. Throughout my childhood, almost every vacation was at the beach. This was the time when schedules and responsibility could wash away and we could enjoy family time. My Dad and I would always have a competition on who would come home with the darkest tan. We often got in trouble for feeding the seagulls from our hotel balcony. It was during this time that I discovered a love for seafood and key lime pie. Life was always so much fun when we were on vacation.

As a child, I was sheltered from the world; bad things happened "out there." Within my four walls, life was simple. My mom was devoted to my dad and we four girls. I always felt especially loved since I was her baby. We spent many hours talking as Mom made the evening meal. She taught me much about life, about being a "good" girl, and about valuing family over everything else. Devoted would be an understatement when describing my Mom. My sisters and I never wanted for much. We only needed each other. I so wanted to be that good girl she was raising; however, I had a desire for more.

'Could I really have it all? What would others think? What would happen if I didn't stay in the neat little box that was expected of me? Can a girl really break the mold?'

I wasn't sure if staying home with kids and maintaining a house was my future. I wanted a career. *'Oh, why do these roaring waves remind me of being so unsettled? Was I to follow the status quo or take that leap of faith and venture out into the world? Did it mean grow up to be a wife and mother or pursue that career?'* I wasn't sure. Being the youngest, I always wanted to please my parents. I knew with certainty they didn't believe women could raise good kids *and* have a career. However, all I knew was that I was a modern girl of the eighties and I desired to "bring home the bacon *and* fry it up in the pan." I wanted to test my boundaries and still make my parents proud.

While surrounded by greatness, the world really is your oyster. How could a young girl ever live in fear when her hero lived right down the hall? Seriously, my perfect world could be falling apart outside our walls as my dad, a police lieutenant, worked throughout the night to keep his family safe. A strong man both physically and intellectually, Dad could scare even the hardest of men. He made it all seem so easy. He would look fear in the eye and overcome it. His stature was intimidating. I remember him telling me that he was offered a position as a tag-team wrestling partner with his later famous older brother. Although flattered, he chose the secure plan for his family. The only thing he cared about was making sure his little girls were safe. He experienced the world so differently than I. I never met the outlaws or the drug dealers.

I remember being startled in the middle of the night when the call came in; yet another drug dealer wanting to sell my undercover Dad drugs. When I would wake up to the ringing phone, yes, the one on the wall, my Dad would tell me everything was fine and, "Go back to bed." Deep down, I knew it wasn't really fine, but I also knew I could sleep peacefully because everything bad happened out there; not in my little world.

You see, much of my life was like the cool, calm water washing away the sand at my feet. In my childlike mind, I lived in the warmth of the sun and the mist of the salty air. *'Oh, if only life could stay like this – if only I could be a hero to my children someday.'*

I struggled with wanting a career *and* being a good parent. My parents made it seem all so easy. We never wanted for much, but, life was different in my day and age. Although I didn't live through the depression, the economy *was* hard. We were caught between booming eras – the technology age and the end of the Cold War – the nothingness in between resulted in a declining economy. I wanted a home, a family, and a career, but didn't know how I would juggle it all. Living on one income seemed impossible, so that meant someone would have to help me raise my kids someday. I wanted to be the perfect Mom and have a lifestyle where I could spoil my family. This was my idea of being a hero; being the perfect working parent.

Leaving the safety net of my family home and leaping into the arms of someone who loved me unconditionally fulfilled my destiny. I wanted nothing more than to be Steve's wife and share life with him. He represented to me everything stable. He was my rock. I was flighty and adventurous; he was calm and confident. I was the dreamer; he was the realist. I couldn't wait to be his Mrs. We were young and in love. Everything was going to be perfect!

Our wedding was magical!

Our fairytale took place on a crisp winter night between Christmas and New Year's. The church was glowing by candlelight and the shimmer of the Christmas tree. As I walked down the aisle in my satin dress holding onto my hero's arm, I was filled with anticipation. I remember looking into my Dad's eyes, taking a deep breath and realizing that life would be different. I would always be his little girl, but now an independent woman forging through this life with the man she loved.

An Ocean Of Love

It was so heartwarming to see everyone I loved right beside me, encouraging me. As I walked toward the front of the church, I saw my sisters in their long burgundy dresses welcoming me to say my vows. The song of the wedding march seemed to fill my heart and soul. With one step in front of the other, our whole future was ahead of us. It was our story to write. My future brothers-in-law, standing beside my soon-to-be husband, looked so proud and dapper in their tuxedos. As my Dad let go of me and kissed me with tears in his eyes, I was united to my soulmate. We may have been young, but we couldn't have been more certain of our future together. I kept wondering what it would be like to love and be loved by my best friend. Although our future was yet to be designed, I knew everything in the world was right and this was God's plan. God had truly blessed us.

As with the changing tide, we are never the same tomorrow as we are today. Becoming a mommy and with the responsibility that title brings, uncertainty became my constant companion. The love for my three sons was overwhelming. *'Would they ever understand the depth of love I had for them? Will I be patient enough, tough enough, or just enough of everything? How do I raise a son into a man? No, wait, how do I raise three sons into men?'*

They were our pride and joy!

Our days were chaotic and filled with energy. We took long walks in the park, threw stones in the water, and played soccer and baseball. We watched more episodes of Barney than I can count. We may not have had the latest and greatest cars or house, but we had each other. I stayed home to raise them and took night classes for a nursing career. Together, Steve and I raised our boys.

I was so proud of the day we could show our kids the big, beautiful ocean they had often heard about. It took years to save up enough money for this beautiful vacation. As I watched my sons splash in the water and get toppled over by the big waves, my heart was proud. I so wanted my kids to love the ocean and the beach as much as I did. I wanted for them to have wonderful memories of family time at the beach – the place where both kids and adults played as children. Steve and I shared a love for our boys that no one could come between. We cherished our little family.

Life was perfect, until—

Suddenly, the waters turned gray and the roaring waves became deafening. The salty air burned my eyes and the air had an uncomfortable chill. The wind hurt my face as I tried to make sense of the pain. My place of peace and comfort felt so cold. Life became so hard!

How could my hero, my stability, my *Dad*, be dying of cancer? What about the vacations, the baseball games, the Christmases he needed to share with my little family? I still needed him to guide me and show my boys how to be a man.

I had to do something to stop his disease.

I couldn't stand back and watch.

I felt so helpless.

Suddenly, my world revolved around test results. One month we would be so grateful for more time and the next stricken with the fear of "What if?". As the *years* went by, we learned to live for today, not knowing if we would lose him, but when Dad would be gone (something that *should* be true for every person), we learned to focus on what really mattered in life:

Each other.

Family.

Faith.

Just like the hundreds of sandcastles I built as a child, my time with my Dad would soon be washed away.

Life became a series of checklists and responsibilities. The little girl in me was a distant memory. If I could just keep all the balls in the air at the same time, I could breathe. Number one, love my children and husband-check; number two, keep the house clean and make the meals-check; number three, watch the kids play sports-check; number four, spend time with my parents and sisters-check; oh, and also study to be a registered nurse for number five.

I could do this!

I needed to be in control. You see, my drug of choice to numb the pain and fear of losing my hero wasn't alcohol or drugs, it was climbing the ladder of success. It seemed to be the perfect solution; obtaining that college degree and helping others took the spotlight off of my stressful life. I could use my new-found skills to help those I loved the most; *'maybe I could cure cancer.'* Not really, but I *could* set the example for my boys that hard work pays off.

Working as an ICU nurse seemed fitting as the cold, sterile environment with all the bells and whistles drowned out my less than perfect life. Distraction really does work, for a while. I loved caring for those who needed me. I could relate to those fearing for their loved one's lives. You see, I now knew what it felt like to say good-bye to someone you love....

The day came when I found myself in a class to which I really didn't want to belong. I had done the impossible. I said good-bye to the man who taught me about life, about work, and about values. He taught me about integrity, and honesty, and how to stand up for what is right. On a day that the world celebrated Thanksgiving, I was in a hospital room holding my hero's hand. Not feeling very thankful, I sat there for hours surrounded by my sisters and Mom; we counted the last few breaths of my Dad's life. He had slipped into a coma after battling an infection – a common side effect of cancer treatments. The burly man he'd been in his youth and mine was now frail and weak. He was tired after a full decade of battling cancer. I knew the struggle he faced at this moment was one he never thought he could endure. He had to let go of his family. Only God could help him now. I so wanted God to end his suffering, but that meant I had to say goodbye to my perfect Daddy here on Earth. I loved him enough to let go.

It was so hard!

If only I could ease this pain for others in just a small way in my new role as an ICU nurse, I guess my experience could be of value. There had to be a reason for this pain. During this season of life, I was so caught up in getting it all done and trying to be the perfect wife, mother, daughter, and sister. It was hard to put one foot in front of the other and move forward. And? I didn't have time to go to my special place. It just wasn't the same. Nothing seemed special. I didn't have time to play or dream or even laugh. *I* wasn't the same.

As the new normal of life settled in, my little family grew. They eventually taught me to laugh again and to see the world through the eyes of a child. They seemed to have grown up so fast. Soon we were planning junior proms, high school graduations, weddings, and baby showers. My meter of success was at an all-time high. My babies grew up into very responsible, good men. My husband still loved me and I was promoted to Director of Nursing at my local hospital. Life should have felt good, so why did I still feel the chill of the salty air? *'Why was the sky still gray?'*

Every day that I went to work, it felt like the sharks of the healthcare industry were telling me that my best would never be enough. It didn't matter how many lives I saved, they still wanted more. The advice I was given was to devote myself to my career since my kids were now the independent young men that I created. *'Why wasn't I happy? Why wasn't I fulfilled?'* No matter how high I climbed the corporate ladder, something was missing. Little did I know that the next, big, drowning wave . . . no. The *tsunami* was about to hit.

The call came in and heard on the other line, "Mom has had a heart attack!"

Oh, Dear God, please wake me from this nightmare. You see, losing one hero was horrible, losing two would be impossible. This independent woman still needed the guidance, support, and love only a Mother could provide. I needed her to share the joy of watching my grandchildren grow. She was there the day they were born. She needed to share her wisdom and her love of family with them.

Losing Mom was *not* on the checklist.

It was *not* in my schedule.

It was *not* part of the plan.

Unfortunately, I couldn't stop this loss, either. This nurse of then-twenty years couldn't fix it. All the education in the world couldn't change the outcome. My Purdue degree couldn't strengthen Mom's heart. I hated the fact that I was a nurse. All I wanted was to be her daughter. I wanted to tell her that she was a perfect Mom. I wanted her to know that it was because of her that I knew how to love my kids. I couldn't awaken from the nightmare and make it all go away. It all happened so fast. I was sitting next to her bed counting those familiar, shallow breaths. Surrounded by her family, her purpose for living, her pride and joy, she breathed her last. *'Oh, that salty air….where is the sun? Where are the Pelicans? Where are the soothing sounds of the ocean?'*

I found solace in these lyrics from Hillsong United's "Oceans (Where Feet May Fail)":

> *"You call me out upon the waters*
> *The great unknown where feet may fall*
> *And there I find You in the mystery*
> *In oceans deep*
> *My faith will stand"*

Suddenly, what I thought was important,' no longer was. The weight of trying to be everything to everyone overcame me. *'Who was I? If I wasn't achieving and striving, then who was I? What type of legacy do I want to leave? What is God's plan, not my plan, for my life?'*

It was time to let go and let God take control. *'I surrender! I'm all yours God! Help me find Me!'*

My world had changed.

◆ ◆ ◆

I believe God's journey is never one of isolation. He sent me the answers to my deepest questions just when I needed them most. It all began with letting go of the past so that I could see a future – a future of encouragement, faith, support, and a little daring. I needed to find myself again. I felt so lost.

As an exercise to overcome the weight of fear and unleash the past, my sister Robyn showed me how to walk the proverbial firewalk. It is the test of courage and evidence of the power of the mind. She knew I needed to let go of the pain so that I could have a brighter future. I was challenged to walk across a bed of hot coals to face my fears. Seriously! I'm not speaking in metaphors! This nurses' mind does not equate walking on hot coals and *not* getting burned. *'Hadn't I had enough pain in my life?'*

My sister knew I needed to believe in myself and my strength. Walking across coals wasn't about fear as much as it was about courage and strength to *face* my fears and doubts. It was about believing in myself. Up to this point in life, I was pretty good at pretending I was in control; others admired my strength. As I walked up to the flaming bed of coals, I felt the doubt, the pain; insecurity paralyzed me. The smell of burning ash and the heat of red burning embers made me weak in the knees. As I looked up and saw my sister ahead of me, her encouragement and support helped me put one foot in front of the other. She knew I needed this. This was how I would have the courage to begin again. Step by step, I walked over the past, the pain, and the fear. Before I knew it, I was looking back at the coals. I emerged with a lighter step, a hope for the future and—most importantly—a belief in myself.

I realized that our minds are extremely powerful. We are capable of so much more than we think. We can endure so much pain and still find beauty. My self-talk was no longer about others' expectations and doubts or about what I'd lost. It was about what I still had, finding fulfillment, and prioritizing my values: faith, family, then business! It was about aligning a vision; a dream for this servant's heart. I found hope and happiness and learned to count my blessings: my beautiful and crazy family including beautiful daughters-in-law, an amazing niece, my adorable pets, my home, my health, and my church. I had so much in life despite this hole in my heart.

I was ready to live again!

God had orchestrated a new, perfect career path; one I never saw coming. A career I could be proud of and excited about. He merged my greatest passion of home and family with the privilege of helping others find a perfect home and create new beginnings. A place where they can create memories and share their dreams. He directed me to a company who shared my values. It was all feeling so natural and right. It felt so "me" for the first time in a long time!

I love to go to my special place every year.

I am thankful for the memories that make it my Heaven on Earth. As I now walk upon the sandy beach, I see the giant footsteps ahead of me, the footprints of my heroes who shaped me into the woman I am today – the daughter, sister, wife, mother, and Naamah (Grandma) I am proud to be. I see the eight tiny footsteps behind me looking for the wisdom and unconditional love that will guide them through the ever-changing tides of life. I feel the warm sun on my back as I hear their small voices giggling and they build their houses of sand. I look beside me and see the footprints of my husband who has always loved and supported me; who has held me up when I didn't think I could stand. I see my amazing sons who value family and hard work – these men who make me laugh and feel proud. My sister who knows what I need before I even know it myself is there, too. I look up and see that I was never alone.

God has given me the courage and strength to find hope and joy. I remain in awe of His strength and beauty as I watch the glistening crest of the next wave and hear its thundering noise pierce my soul. I study my own footprint and realize that I am blessed. My mission in life is to inspire others. You see, I now know who I am. I am my father's little girl, my mother's daughter and The Father's chosen one. I do not live in fear. I know where I am going. Living a life by God's design, I have faith!

◆ ◆ ◆

My prayer is that my journey helps others create a life they love, to be true to themselves, and to ride their own waves. Although life will knock us down, we are so much stronger than we think. Our heroes have paved the way, leaving their footprints to mark the trail.

It all begins with that special place where you find your true self – a place where you can just be you and not some expectation you set for yourself. It is a place of joy and contentment – a place where life seems so clear. It's not about titles, degrees, or reputations, it's about living your life! It's where legacies are born and life's deepest questions are answered.

Where is the place where you will find your true self?

When you find it, "Welcome home, my friend. Welcome home."

"A calm sea never made a

skilled sailor."

~ Franklin D. Roosevelt

Brad Parent is a life-long entrepreneur, having founded or successfully built more than a handful of companies during his career. Brad's true passion in life is helping others realize and exceed their stretch goals, and he is currently doing so as the founder of Simplified Realty Group—a division of Keller Williams. Brad knows what courage it takes to face life's painful tragedies of all types and flourish on the other side. Along with being a thoughtful husband and proud father of three, Brad loves the beach, Canadian fishing and hunting, and also enjoys boating, golf, and snowmobiling. Learn more at: **bradparent.com**.

BENEATH THE SURFACE

Brad Parent

◆ ◆ ◆

A aron Rogahn, Ken Schremp, and Eric Dixon were in the first floatplane. Matt Meister, Lance White, Garland "Boo" Bond, and I were in the second floatplane.

It was so very rare to have a group of seven guys who all got along well, didn't annoy each other, and looked forward to spending endless days and nights just hanging out.

Aaron was a head turning, handsome, young (fifteen years my junior), man with a warm smile; he was full of life and was a magnetic force when entering a room, but always focused on everyone else – a rare combination. Despite our age difference, we became fast, best, instant, lifelong, bonded friends.

Eric was a friend and a man who loved nature and our Canadian fishing expeditions.

Ken was almost always happy and smiling and had a disarming way about him; you just know he wouldn't hurt a fly. The only time I ever saw Ken get mad was after he hit three consecutive tee shots out of bounds while we were golfing "up north." Then, he shrugged it off, took a sip of his Sprecker Dopple Bock, and said, "Come on, Brad, let's go find those crappy shots," with his smile already back on his face.

I can still see the faces of my three friends in my mind; but this is the story about the last time I saw them in person.

◆ ◆ ◆

The trip had morphed over the course of almost twenty years, but it began because Ken and I grew tired of "regular" fishing in the state of Wisconsin, which—by many people's standards—is *known* for good fishing. Having grown up spending countless boring hours not catching anything when fishing with my dad, I was especially excited about catchin' . . . *not* fishin', so—after attending a few All Canada Shows—we decided to try a fly-in Canadian fishing adventure. It only takes one fly-in trip to become hooked, because catching was *so* much more fun than fishing.

The trip started taking shape in the dead of winter when Ken and I collected everyone's deposits and began the process of firming up travel plans for late May. There were always a few emails here and there during that time, but the real build up began about six to eight weeks out, when Ken would send his big list of stuff to bring for the expedition. He was always the one priming the pump that would get the string of emails started between the members of the group.

Ken and Eric enjoying a fishing day.

Ken knew how to be a great friend, whether it was weight lifting and racquetball three times a week, hunting, snowmobiling, ice fishing, golf, or just getting together at his island cabin in northern Wisconsin. He loved to find hole-in-the-wall places, have a drink, and talk with the locals everywhere. He was a true outdoorsman and a great teacher for those of us who didn't have the benefit of a father teaching us the lessons of the outdoors. Ken would get some random picture of a 200-pound catfish and send it to everyone saying, "this looks like something Boo would catch back home in Arkansas!"

Not exactly 200 pounds, but still a nice string of walleye for Aaron.

I remember another email that said, "Do not open the attached picture if you have a weak stomach." After opening the picture(of course!)—it was a photo of a few guys circled around a twelve-pack of broken beer bottles on the ground. The email jokes, jabs, and funny photos would get around fast and furious those last few weeks. Getting ready for the trip and planning for it was where the fun of the expedition actually began. As we counted down the days, the anticipation of the good times ahead would build to a crescendo.

"The boys" took two trucks from Wisconsin to carry all the gear for the trip. The trucks were always loaded to the gills and, as Matt liked to say, "Canada is all about hauling shit."

Matt wasn't disgruntled about it, but he definitely liked to point it out; to him it was just a fact of life that went along with the Canadian fishing experience that he has observed over the years. Since he was a big, strong, burly type of guy, he got to handle the heavier stuff like Aaron's overstuffed and over-packed enormous duffle bag.

We haul stuff into the trucks.

We haul stuff to the docks.

We load the planes.

We unload the planes on the outpost cabin dock.

We haul stuff up the winding path to the cabin.

We haul stuff back down the path to the boats.

We haul stuff to the shore for shore lunches.

We haul stuff off the boats at the end of the day.

Then—the next morning—we hauled gas and everything we needed to the boats for the day. Matt was right. It *was* all about hauling shit.

The best part of having the same group of guys every year, though, was that we had a pretty good system down. Everyone chipped in and all the work was fun; it was just part of being in the wilderness by ourselves. We had to bring in all our food, drinks, camping, and fishing gear for the week. Although we stayed in a cabin, we still needed to bring sleeping bags. We never knew what kind of weather we were going to run into up there in Ontario, Canada.

We'd seen days where it had been sunny and seventy and then, thirty minutes later, *boom*. It could be storming and the temperature could drop thirty degrees or more. If the sun wasn't out it was chilly and the nights were always cold in May. Some nights we'd have a

Eric, Ken, Aaron, and Brad enjoy a shoreside lunch before it gets cool.

bonfire outside near the lake and the show the Northern Lights put on always made being outside worthwhile.

But there was no better feeling than watching the floatplane taxi away from the dock knowing that the only people left out there in the middle of nowhere was the group of close friends doing life together.

When Aaron, Matt, and I picked up Lance in southern Wisconsin, the first thing Aaron said to Lance was that he couldn't wait for the "initiation" Lance was going to have to go through. Lance had been admitted to the club for the first time this trip and he was

Garland "Boo" Bond (above). Ken and Eric fish in Schrempy's stream (below).

excited! I played along with it and told Lance that I was sorry I forgot to share that little tidbit of information earlier. From there, the four of us traveled to Minnesota where we met Ken and Eric who had left a day early to get some fishing in at Pelican Lake, Minnesota. Aaron was the first out of the truck and was talking to both Ken and Eric when Lance walked

up to them. This was the first time that Lance had met Eric and he picked up where Aaron had left off, asking about the initiation. We spent the entire drive catching up with one another as a group and having a good time.

We were in two trucks and, since Boo lived in Washington D.C., he usually flew into central Wisconsin, Duluth, Minnesota, or International Falls, Minnesota where we picked him up and the party would begin. That year, we rendezvoused in International Falls and then crossed the border into Canada. The border was where we always got our Canadian beer for the trip and other last-minute provisions before the three-hour drive took us up to Pickerel Arms Base Camp in Sioux Lookout, Ontario.

We had a great time catching up with one another during the drive and there was no absence of joking and ribbing one another all the way. Each truck had a walkie-talkie to stay in touch and keep the stories flowing between the vehicles. Although we hadn't been together as a group since the year before, we picked up like it had only been a week. Somehow, this never got old; the incredible rock formations during the drive, an occasional gangly moose sighting trotting parallel to us in the steep ditches, and the glass-like lakes and ponds that were around almost every curve were always inspiring.

A few days before embarking on our trip, we had found out that the group going to Fawcett Lake the previous week had not been able to fly in because there was still too much ice on the lake. The previous week's weather had consisted of sub forty degrees and snow flurries. We had just found out the day before our trip began that the ice was melting and flowing off the lake and that we *would* be able to fly in to Fawcett. It was a beautiful sunny seventy-one-degree day and we were all excited at the recent turn of weather. We kept commenting on our good fortune for the weather to break just in time for our arrival.

We got into Sioux Lookout around 3:00 P.M., which was the earliest we had ever gotten there. Normally we stayed at base camp on the day of our arrival and were flown to the remote lake at first light the next morning, but it seemed like something was different when we pulled into base camp.

There was a lot of activity around camp, as the beginning of fishing season was moving into full swing. We checked in with Lee, who ran the camp, and we got our fishing licenses. There was still plenty of daylight left as sunset wouldn't be until another six hours. As luck would have it, Lee told us the two float planes would be back in time to take us in that afternoon instead of having to wait until the first flight out the next morning! The floatplanes only fly during daylight. As if we needed anything to get us more excited! Now we would have so much extra fishing time and another bonfire night at the lake!

We still had a little extra time to kill before they were going to fly us in and Matt asked if anyone wanted to go up the road a few miles to a camp named Frog Rapids to pick up some T-shirts. Boo, Lance, and I joined in to pick up some sort of souvenir. As we headed up the hill on the dirt road from base camp and turned onto the main road toward Frog Rapids, we were surprised to see the first Beaver (floatplane) returning from one of the outposts so soon. Everything seemed to run late in the bush after the first run of the day, but it looked like both planes would be at base camp sooner than expected, so we figured we'd better take care of our errand and hurry back. We got our shirts and, as we were walking back to the truck, Matt ran into an acquaintance from his hometown in Reedsburg, Wisconsin. What were the odds?

Matt chatted with his friend for a few minutes and then we hopped in the truck. Just as we were arriving back at camp at 6:15 P.M., we saw Ken, Eric, and Aaron pulling away from the dock in the first plane. I felt bad not getting back in time to help them load the plane and be on it with them. We waved at each other and Aaron yelled at us from the co-pilot seat to bring the CDs from the truck. The four of us stood on the dock, watched them taxi toward the middle of the lake, and power up with a long takeoff into that untamed, blue, northern sky.

I was with good friends on the dock, the air was pure and perfect, we were surrounded by the lake and forest, and our first group looked magnificent disappearing into the horizon. It was a picture-perfect day and hard to get a better start to a guys' fishing trip.

Aaron, Ken, and Eric had loaded everything that was in Ken's truck onto that first plane except for some extra cases of soda, beer, and water that were set-aside on the dock. We knew the second Beaver would be coming soon, so

Ken, Aaron, and Brad on a Beaver during a previous trip.

Matt backed his truck down to the dock and we unloaded everything while waiting for the second plane. Matt, Boo, and I had flown with the same pilot from the second Beaver, Fred, the previous year, so we were glad to see him. We loaded up the plane and also left some of our provisions on the dock, so they could bring them to us on the "check stop" that would occur a couple of days later. We took off about one hour behind the first plane.

The fly-in camps are spread across several lakes and it was ninety-seven miles north, or about an hour flight from base camp to Fawcett Lake. From the air, a lot of time is spent looking out a plane window and taking in the amazing views because it's too loud to talk much while flying in a Beaver. Sometimes, we crack open an ice-cold Labatt's Blue beer and enjoy the scenery while trying to spot moose.

It was a great aerial view with the Cat River system connecting all the lakes and there was as much water as land to be seen up there. There was a ton of timber everywhere, but we could see where some swaths of it had been cut, as well as the logging roads that led into parts of the

View from the floatplane.

forest. As we continued heading north, the roads and logging dissipated and it was only the great, raw country as it had been for centuries.

During the last five to ten minutes of the flight, we began to see a gradual increase of ice where all the coves and small bays were iced over. We were expecting to see some ice, but it was an unusual sight to see that much of it at that time of year. We knew we were getting close and became super excited as we flew over the far end of the of a lake and saw everyone's favorite

spot...Three Falls. It was a spot where three huge waterfalls converge, forming a swirling eddy of fish-filled water. The bald eagles even hung out there due to the abundance of walleye pike and we all loved to feed them and take video of the huge birds grabbing fifteen-inch walleyes with their talons right out of the water in front of our boats.

The whole group by a small waterfall.

We came upon the main part of the lake and did our usual fly-by, spotting a line of ice and then plenty of open water, as we flew over the dock and cabin. We didn't see any signs of the guys from the first plane on the dock. They must have been in the cabin trying to get all their rods rigged. We would have to hurry to catch up and be ready to head out and catch a few that evening...just because we could.

We circled over the back end of the lake, descended into the center of the mirrored surface, and Fred gave us the smoothest landing in glass-like water, then taxied to the dock. We expected to see some sign that they were there—a duffle, an ice chest, a stray case of beer; something they would have left on the dock. All the boats were docked, too. After tying the Beaver up to the dock, we ran into the cabin, but it was empty with no sign of the guys from the first plane. We ran back down to our plane and told the pilot there wasn't any sign of them. Fred asked if they could be playing a big joke on us; but none of us believed that was the case.

Fred's face dropped and his expression immediately changed to something more serious. Fred could not use his radio on the water and needed to get up in the air to call base camp and the other airborne planes to see if the first Beaver made a stop at one of the other outposts. He took off saying that maybe they had some trouble and turned back or had to land on another lake. He said most likely he would have them at the lake with us (and the rest of our stuff) in the morning. All of us felt that he was right and we would be seeing them in the morning. We took most of our gear up to the cabin wondering what kind of wild adventure we would be hearing from the guys after they made it to the cabin in the morning.

While getting settled into the cabin, we realized that all the food and drinks were on the first plane along with the satellite radio. It was past 8:00 P.M. and we began discussing what we were going to do for dinner. Fish was the obvious choice since they were so easy to catch at any time of the day or night. Lance and I headed over to one of the fishing spots close the cabin and tried to catch something for dinner. Matt and Boo headed out to a second spot that was more toward the remaining ice that was still on the north side of the lake. We were mainly curious to see if we could get through the ice flows to other sections of water that were connected through the river system.

A race to hit the best fishing spots!

We each got into our respective fishing boats and headed out. Lance and I stopped shortly and had a line in the water right away. We could see Matt and Boo putting along and checking out the ice line toward the area we had just flown over an hour ago. After about five minutes in the boat, Matt pointed over to the ice and shouted to Boo that it looked like there was an ice heave at the edge of the line of ice a little farther away. It was dead calm and quiet, and we could hear the faint sound of their motor and Matt's voice carry across the water. We watched them scan the horizon where Matt was pointing as we waited for the first of hundreds of bites we most certainly were going to experience over the next few days.

As Boo focused on the image from the front of the boat, he yelled back to Matt, "it looks like it has two parallel lines and looks man-made."

Lance and I weren't that interested in fishing right at the moment since the boys seemed to be finding something cooler over by them. We also wanted to check out the ice situation to make sure we could get through the next morning before we decided where to fish, so we headed toward the other guys. Boo was kneeling on the seat leaning forward for a better view and, as they got closer, he realized it wasn't an ice heave. It was shiny—not the good kind of shiny—the kind of shiny that doesn't belong in the Canadian wilderness. As they closed in, more of the outline was discernable and it looked like a giant ship propeller half submerged in the water. Then, Boo connected the end of those two parallel lines running toward what looked like a ship propeller. It was right then that he realized it was a plane . . . upside down; he gasped; his heart pounding while struggling to get the words out.

He turned to Matt in the back of the boat and screamed, "It has to be our first plane upside down in the water!"

Lance and I could hear what Boo said ringing out over the water. We saw his words register on Matt whose face dropped, and then he said, "Oh God. Oh God, no."

I hit the throttle to get us over there as quickly as I could, saying to myself, '*God I cannot believe this is happening. This can't be happening; not here; not now; not to us; not to them. That can't be their plane. They have to be okay. They're somewhere around here.*'

When we finally got up to the anomaly of nature, we saw it was definitely a plane upside down in the water. One pontoon was crossed over the other making a V-shape at the back and that was what made the parallel lines. The big, oblong-shaped rudders at the end of the pontoons were also crossed over making a propeller shape.

Suddenly, it hit us. Everything that seemed so good about the Canadian wilderness now felt remote and brutal. It was a surreal moment as we tried to comprehend everything that was happening while not wanting to believe it at the same time.

Matt pulled their boat up to the plane and we all began yelling, making noise and calling out our friends' names.

Matt got close enough for Boo to bang on one of the pontoons as Boo kept saying, "We have to do something! We have to do something!"

We were close to the middle part of the lake with the ice line about 100 yards out and the closest shore about 500 yards away. Meanwhile, as we circled the boat, we could see a strut, or a little bit of the plane body beneath the surface. We also couldn't see too far into the normally clear but now tannin-stained water as full daylight was going away. After a couple of circles and without notice, Boo jumped in the water to see if he could find any sign of them. It was against everyone's advice.

So many things went through my head in those few seconds. I especially wondered if he would see anyone down there, but also whether Boo's decision would worsen this already horrific situation. Matt leaned over the boat to hold Boo's hand while he was in the water because we were worried about the icy temperature and any other dangers down there. Boo looked around, but really couldn't see much and he couldn't make out the shape of the cabin to get to a window. He came back up for air and said he was going to have to go back down, but would have to go deeper. He tried getting down to the cabin to find a door or window or anything that would give us some new information. As he was down there, he became disoriented. It seemed that it should have been simple, but parts of the plane that he expected to be in a certain place weren't there. He couldn't visualize where he was in relation to rest of the plane. He wasn't down for any great length of time, but the water wasn't clear because of the fuel and oil which was coating and burning his eyes at the same time that the water was getting murky and difficult to see in as he searched.

We all wanted him out of the water and kept yelling at him, "Get your ass back in the boat before you freeze to death!"

Boo was shivering by this time from being in the icy water. He came up for air and crawled onto one of the pontoons to get out of the lake and rest. The pontoon he was resting on began to gurgle and air bubbles came to the surface. We were afraid that he had just sunk the rest of the plane with his weight and this was the worst thing we could have ever done, especially not having any idea how deep the lake was in that area. He got off the pontoon and back in the water to come back in the boat. The wreckage of the plane began listing his way and we were afraid that it may continue to tilt and sink, sucking Boo down with it to the bottom.

Matt grabbed him and dragged him back in the boat.

While Boo was under water, we had already planned on Matt taking Boo back to the cabin so he would be ok. Matt tried to get him warmed up by the wood stove. Laying in front of the wood stove, curled into a ball, his whole body violently shivering, Boo screamed aloud in the empty cabin, "This can't be happening, it just can't be!"

Lance and I, still on the lake, began a systematic search of the area. Eric was a survivalist; surely they had enough warning to get out of the plane. They had to be somewhere . . . *anywhere*. Maybe they were unconscious; we had to find them before it was too late. None of this felt possible. As we gradually searched in expanding circles from the plane and yelled out for the Eric, Ken and Aaron, I reflected on less chaotic times with my best friend, Aaron.

Aaron and I had bought our first identical Yamaha four wheelers together. There was another time when he "caught" my five-year-old son, Carson, who was rolling backward down a steep and tree rutted path in the woods by blocking him with his machine. I was the only non-family member at Aaron's wedding, because—to one another—we *were* family. How much fun we had with my daughter, Ashton, and her friend at Lambeau Field for her first Packer game.

Still lost in thought, I spotted something floating on the water about twenty-five yards away. Since it was after 10:00 P.M. by now and the long Canadian rays of daylight were beginning to wane, it was difficult to make out what it was. I know what my mind was preparing me for; was it one of my best buddies in the world floating on the water? It seemed like slow motion as we circled closer. I was painfully reluctant, but turned the six-foot long, dark blue object over. It was Aaron's large duffle bag. I couldn't pull it into the boat myself, but I was determined to hold onto this piece of Aaron, so Lance and I nearly capsized our boat getting it in over the side. As we looked around, as if appearing out of nowhere, there were full beer cans, tackle boxes, coolers, and other gear scattered across the lake and floating on the water. Where had it all been earlier? How had we not spotted the debris? The surface wasn't smooth, after all.

I grabbed Ken's blue and white cooler and put it in our boat without reason. For the next couple of hours we drove from one item in the water to another. By this time, Matt had come back out to the site of the plane to help us search. The three of us just kept praying out loud and yelling their names.

After not seeing anyone or hearing any response, we headed toward the nearest shore on the east side of the lake. After not seeing anyone or hearing any response, we headed toward the other shore. *'Where were my friends? They had to be on the shore somewhere. Eric would have made sure of that.'*

Matt went back to the cabin to check on Boo; he got a floating buoy and LED flashlight to mark the plane's position in case it sank. He sank the buoy near the back of the plane's tail and placed the light on one of the pontoons facing skyward. Everyone continued searching the shores and the water while the long twilight faded to darkness.

Each of us played our role. Boo, compelled to do something, acted without regard for his own safety. Matt was careful, minding Boo, marking the spot of the wreckage with buoy and flashlight. I systematically searched with intentionality, because they surely had to be somewhere. And Lance was steady. This was not the initiation he signed up for.

It became less useful to conduct the search in the deep blackness and it was dangerous being out on the lake. We had spotted several darks rocks just above the water surface earlier and there was no way we could see them in the dark. Everything became very inky and very dark . . . very quickly. That night was a new moon, so it provided no real light; we were in the middle of nowhere; and the search was not turning up anything new. Considering all of these circumstances, we begrudgingly went back to the cabin around midnight. Boo was suffering from hypothermia and the fire was not cooperating in the wood stove. He was freezing, so Lance grabbed the shelves that were intended for the kitchen wall, and side-kicked them into kindling-sized pieces. We all made sure after that to keep the fire roaring to thaw our friend out.

We collected our thoughts, each of us running down our own mental checklists wondering if there was something we might have missed . . . something we could do. We desperately wanted to find our buddies. There didn't seem to be anything else we could have done at that time, but waiting with no answers was torture.

Around 1:00 A.M., a large plane with four propellers flew overhead and Matt, Lance, and I ran down to the dock signaling SOS with flashlights to the plane. They circled overhead for about thirty minutes before flying away. They came back on two additional occasions and we signaled from the dock each time with no response - no communication - no signals - nothing at all; and no help for our friends that we thought may still be alive somewhere, if they had been able to jump from the plane prior to impact. The flashlight remained lit on the pontoon throughout the longest night Boo, Lance, Matt, and I had ever experienced.

Shortly after 4:00 A.M., the first light of the morning began to appear and we all headed back to the lake to start searching the shores again by boat. The same type of search plane as the one we'd seen in the night returned around 5:30 A.M. and Boo and Matt happened to be closest to the crash location, so they went to where the crash was and signaled SOS to the plane from their boat. The plane was flying low and circled several times. The ramp in the back of the plane opened and we could see someone standing in the opening. The person in the opening parachuted an emergency radio to us and we were able to make contact at last.

We told them that we had found the floatplane and it was marked.

We told them that we had not seen any sign of our friends and did not know for certain if they were in the plane.

We told them that we were okay and did not need any immediate assistance.

The Beaver that originally brought us to the lake returned shortly after we made contact. It went to the dock so we went to meet the pilot in the floatplane. We continued answering questions from the Search and Rescue team in the air, until they told us they were getting low on fuel and would have to leave.

We contacted the Ontario Province Police (OPP), via a satellite phone that had been brought on the floatplane and the police told us they would take over the search and rescue efforts; they wanted us to leave.

Not a chance.

Boo, Lance, Matt and I refused, but were later actually ordered to leave. They told us they would not have divers in the water for quite some time. *'Why not?'* Eventually, defeated, we packed up some of our gear and decided to leave with the floatplane. The four of us flew back to base camp at Sioux Lookout, still not sure what had happened . . . or if our buddies were okay.

In a tragedy, information gets communicated incorrectly and immediately; this was no different. A wife of one of the guy's had called up to base camp to make sure we made it into camp. She had not received a call from him as had normally happened. She was told that I had been in the plane that went down. By the time we made it back to base camp, my wife had already received a call that I had been in the lost plane. She was devastated and in shock. Her mother had died when she was a five-year-old little girl . . . in a plane crash. Now her husband, too?

As soon as we made it back to camp, I called my wife and family. Then, I had to move onto more difficult communications when I began calling my best friends' wives to give them the unfortunate news. Driving our friends' vehicles back to their families is an eerie experience and we were all in shock for weeks, months, and—for me, personally—years after the accident.

Several excruciating days later, when the divers did finally get to the wreckage, they confirmed that the pilot and our three friends were still strapped into their seats.

The unthinkable became even more of a reality.

My good lifelong friends: Aaron Rogahn, Ken Schremp, and Eric Dixon.

The trip was Eric (Dix) Dixon's, Ken (Schrempy) Schremp's, and Aaron (Junior) Rogahn's last expedition. It remains a struggle to comprehend that it ended in such a way. Everything that seemed to be going so well for us, ended so completely wrong. It is difficult for Boo, Lance, Matt, and I to make sense of any of it and, while we try to cope with the loss of our friends, we can only imagine the degree of loss our friends' families have gone through. If our love for them could bring them back, they would be here today. And if there were still a chance our rescue efforts would find them, we would still be up there searching the cold, fuel-filled waters of Fawcett Lake.

From time to time, I still wonder. '*Why did I go for a t-shirt? I had three of them already from years' past? If Matt hadn't run into his friend from Wisconsin, would I have been on the first plane with my best friends? Would it have changed anything?*'

As I go through life, I realize it is almost impossible for anyone to get through this journey without something significantly negative having an impact. Yes, tragedies—it appears--are unavoidable. And, although they can seemingly bring a person to their knees, they are an integral part of our experience. They are part of what makes us who we are.

Eric, Ken, and Aaron went down that day.

But, in the years before then, I knew, loved, and learned from them and it made me a better man, today. I still sometimes laugh remembering Ken's jokes and everything he taught me about deer hunting and the outdoors. When I pack for a trip, I can hear Eric telling me to, "always remember your waterproof matches." And I'll never forget Aaron's fearless sense of adventure and enthusiasm to do or try anything.

Their lives left a stamp on my own legacy and I know that all I do has a piece of them in it. When I hug my family, I hold on a second longer because my friends don't have that option. When I make a business transaction, it is honest and fair because my buddies were. When I close my eyes each night, I rescue all the good I can in the world to take with me into the next days because I couldn't rescue my good friends.

And in these little and big things, they are still here, not in the turbulent polluted chaos of life, but as a calm but lively presence deep beneath the surface of me like the great expanse hiding under the glass-like face of a peaceful lake.

"Mind set is like a muscle;

to build its strength and

endurance, you must train it

daily."

~ Terri Lewis

Terri Lewis contributed quotes and section introductions throughout "KNOWING WORTH." She is lifelong resident of southeastern Wisconsin and a proud mom, wife, daughter, friend, and—since 2003—successful realtor. Terri is a natural connector and entrepreneur. She believes in the power of faith and dreaming big. She strives to live a purpose-driven life inspired by Maya Angelou's words that "People may not remember exactly what you said, but they will never forget how you made them feel." Adding "Author" to her title has been a "pie in the sky" lifelong goal and she is absolutely thrilled and truly honored to be a part of this book project. Visit **TerriLewis.com** for more information.

◆ ◆ ◆

"A legacy is not something you leave FOR people, it's something you leave IN people."

~ *Peter Strople*

All proceeds of Knowing Worth will go to KW Cares and other worthy causes.

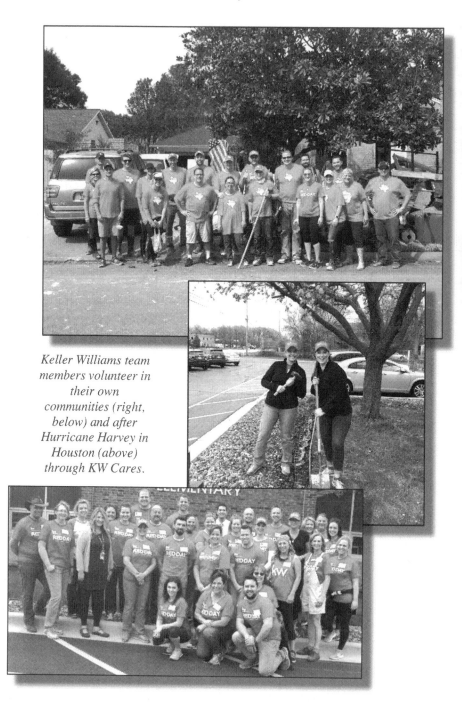

Keller Williams team members volunteer in their own communities (right, below) and after Hurricane Harvey in Houston (above) through KW Cares.

Philanthropy is based on voluntary action for the common good. It's a valued tradition of giving that is primary to a better quality of life. Keller Williams associates fundraise for KW Cares in order to provide emergency financial assistance and grants for those experiencing hardship from sudden emergencies and prolonged tragedies.

KW Cares is at the heart of the Keller Williams philanthropy culture in action, finding and serving the higher purposes of business through charitable giving in the communities where KW associates live and work.

Since its inception, KW Cares has sent money, supplies, gifts, and volunteers to natural disasters around the country, to families battling cancer and other illnesses, and to local and regional schools, gardens, and food pantries. They have given grants to cover medical treatments, emergency expenses, and recovery efforts. They have paid for and helped lead efforts to put service animals with those in need, have led efforts to find organ and blood donations, and held blood drives. KW Cares has served family and friends of Keller Williams, communities where they have offices, and the nation when it is in need. They have served these individuals and communities, often at the sacrifice of their own paychecks and always in pursuit of a legacy worth leaving.

Visit and learn more about KW Cares at **www.kwcares.org**.

"Your story could be the key

that unlocks someone else's

prison. Share it."

~ Toby Mac

38851061R00096

Made in the USA
Lexington, KY
12 May 2019